Second Edition: August 2024

Printed in the United States of America

Questions? Email qr@eshlepper.com

ISBN#: 978-1-960282-05-7

See also:

eBook on Amazon Kindle Marketplace

Full-color edition: 978-1-960282-06-4

Hardcover: Coming soon

1. Acknowledgements

If I had to name the thing that this project has most to appreciate for its success, I'd have to say, unfortunately, *The COVID-19 virus.*

As I penned and prepared the first edition for publication, throughout 2013, most of the friends upon whom I called for comments or discussed the project with were wary; *what on earth is a QR Code? What could there possibly be to say about it at book length?*

Naturally, I simply shrugged off such feedback as the ignorance of those who were simply *not the target audience for such a feature.* But, time proved them entirely correct. The QR Code craze that characterized 2012-2013 was destined to be short-lived. Despite the good reception the book received (from a select group of marketing professional, but certainly not the broader public), it seemed that the QR Code was indeed a fad that wouldn't be returning. It seemed that the craze had run its course.

But, clearly the little-barcode-that-could had other plans. Owing to some powerful champions, such as the United States Postal Service[1], that saw great potential and invested energy and money in promoting the technology, it limped on.

But the most potent force that revived the glowing embers of the QR Code's popularity was the COVID-19 pandemic, which caused a paradigm shift in the way the world operated. Suddenly, the basics of business were turned on end.

Unless you've been living under a rock for the past five years, you know that the COVID pandemic has revived QR Codes in ways that would have been impossible a few years prior. Under what other conditions would exchanging physical objects have become nearly impossible for so long? Under what circumstances would consumers eschew paper forms or restaurant menus? What would it take for consumers and businesses to suddenly, en masse, favor interacting visually and through glass partitions.

Just a few examples of the paradigm shift:

- *Traditional local businesses, that had relied on their physical anchors, had to transition from brick-and-mortar, to pure online customer experiences.*
- *Restaurants had to figure out how to put menus in the hands of their customers, without customers touching them.*
- *Basic business materials like business cards became suspect.*
- *Customers had to be able to browse conveniently and navigate directly to what they needed.*
- *Generally, most business processes had to change as they evolved into the new "touchless" service concept.*
- *The world shifted to interactions via remote methods, or where required, from behind glass partitions.*

The QR Code was uniquely suited to this. There was certainly a multi-year lull in QR Code popularity, but it is back in force – and certainly here to stay.

Philip Warbasse, of Warbasse Designs & Print2D.com, who shared comments on QR Codes early on. He's a rare breed, and contributed valuable comments, adding his company's philosophy, as well as images and documentation. I recall that the day our interview was scheduled, he was home sick: but still remembered our appointment and was ready to go. Many thanks!

http://www.Print2D.com

To the staff at QRStuff.com, whose excellent and unique service has not only been the backbone of some of my most complicated campaigns using QR Codes, but whose altogether unique features have fueled many amazing things that never could have been possible otherwise. They have also graciously provided permissions to reprint content from their white papers, research and other website content & creative in this book... and have asked little in return beyond a link and citation. Good on ya, mates!

http://www.QRStuff.com

To George Williams, for generously sharing his dissertation on QR Codes; your careful documentation has been a very useful source of primary research sources, and your exhaustive listing of potential uses of QR Codes is prodigious.

To Mrs. Bryant, my 10th grade English teacher. What can I say? I really gave you a tough time! How did you ever tolerate my penchant for working obscene, foot-noted expletives-disguised-as-acronyms into my essays? Your tutelage was late in sinking home, and I am today an acolyte of your cult of your "four fatal flaws" grading process. You may un-cap your red pen in 3… 2… 1…

And of course, most of all to my amazing wife Tsezariya, who has been infinitely patient with me while I tinkered, worked late into the night developing some new PHP class or jQuery marvel, stopped dead in the middle of main street to scan every QR Code I encounter, horded every QR Code-bearing piece of media I run across, and most especially for allowing me free reign to use her business as a guinea pig for every experimental social media, marketing or response tracking technique that occurs to me, from tracking-cookie based remarketing, voice-based marketing, social, inbound, email, outdoor, and concepts that don't even have fixed names yet: But, at the end of the day, marketing can only do so much: Your cooking is the better mousetrap that has the world beating a path to your door.

---

[1] *USPS has gone so far as to have ongoing bulk business mail discounts for mailers who employ QR Codes in their direct mail solicitations.*

2. Disclaimers

This book contains information about various Mobile Marketing technologies, including QR Codes, and describes their use and application for marketing. This information is provided as-is and with no warrantee. It is provided for informational use only, and no portion thereof is provided as, nor shall be considered legal or professional advice of any sort.

Information herein is believed accurate at the original date of publication, but no guarantees are made or shall be implied as to the accuracy of this information, nor its appropriateness or fitness for any specific purpose. As this document discusses new and emerging technologies, there is no way to predict what future laws and practices may come to supersede, proscribe, contraindicate, or outright prohibit the practice of ideas proposed herein.

Laws vary from locale to locale, and it is the responsibility of each individual, corporation, or entity to research the laws for all jurisdictions in which they plan to conduct operations of any sort, and seek competent legal counsel to ensure that all practices and measures undertaken are in fact in full compliance with local law. This book is written for North American audiences, and it must be acknowledged that privacy laws in Germany and many parts of the E.U. already constrain a great deal of the tracking & analysis technologies that are reliable standards for U.S. businesses. Each reader is advised to assess the practicality and permissibility of these strategies individually, and always seek to balance business data, marketing and response-tracking needs with individual privacy.

Use of this manual constitutes agreement that the author, publisher, distributors, and all parties associated with the production and sale of this manual are released from any and all liability for damages that may result from the application of any ideas presented in this document, without limitation.

All trademarks and trade names mentioned herein are the property of their respective copyright owners, including but not limited to those listed in the trademarks appendix, and are mentioned purely for illustrative purposes, in discussing players on the field of QR Code use; their mention should not be construed as to suggest any relationship, partnership, or licensing arrangement with the author or publisher. Rather, the same is expressly disclaimed.

The author has received no compensation from any of the companies whose services have been recommended or discussed herein. Many of such companies have affiliate marketing arrangements, referral incentive programs, etc, for their products, and as such it is conceivable that the author might at some future time receive compensation from one or more of said companies (quite unlikely, but a guy can hope, no?). Although all comments and recommendations herein are provided purely on the merits of each service, the author in all cases reserves the right to monetize such arrangements in any way and without reservation. However, this has not been done… yet.

Note that previous editions direct readers to visit **http://qru.ms** for samples and demonstrations. Subscriptions to the site are no longer offered. References to the same have been removed, except where their absence would have been disruptive to the flow of the discussion.

3. Foreword

To you, the brave, boot-strapping business-owner on a budget, or the hard-working marketing consultant needing to keep up with new technologies: You are the target audience for this title. Not the big budget big guys who have all the tools, hold all the cards, and know all the tricks; although many could learn a thing or two from the thorough lashing they get in these pages.

It's for the learner, the do-er, the Do-It-Yourself-er: the entrepreneur who's like the proverbial soldier: short on everything except enemies; short on time, capital, and all else, save determination & moxie. This book is for you, and the goal is to ramp you up to world-class levels of expertise quickly, painlessly, and get you performing shoulder-to-shoulder with the X-Marts and and Y, Incs in at least one area, today. With a bag of tricks to make them jealous, and little-guy agility they can never match, this information is sure to be a marketing game-changer for you... over and beyond simply the application of QR Codes. **This book is intended to be a complete program for applying QR Codes to your every marketing need, quickly and easily, at whatever level you're comfortable pursuing it.**

What's more, I'd very much like to hear back from readers about how they feel about this book. After reading, please take the time to use the links at the end of the book to visit various pages that sell this book online and rate it, write a review, and share your opinions with others (read: Amazon, Amazon & Amazon). I feel confident that I've done a thorough job, and have made this more than worth the money you paid. Frankly, after reviewing most of the offerings out there, and discussing the experiences with readers of the first edition, I have absolute confidence that this is the best and only book out there that covers this topic in its entirety. So, if you feel that this book was worth the cover price, by all means tell others about it; it helps me sell more copies, and punishes the host of cheats selling 16-page pamphlets (including title, copyright, references, index, blank pages & 20-point type) for $20+ on Amazon, claiming to be books on QR Code marketing. Chutzpah! It's an insult to serious professionals who put months of research and work into an enterprise like this. And by all means, give them a fair and unbiased review, while you're at it. As I re-review and update this in July of 2024, having watched the first few months of the AI explosion, I can only image the appalling quality of materials out there that are being regurgitated, plagiarized and zhuzhed by AI – I've certainly seen the absurd *get rich quick selling books generated by AI* ads, and suspect it's quite a jungle out there.

This book is the product of years of practice and research at stretching the boundaries of what's possible with this technology (still haven't found the limits), and more than six months of constant work dedicated to the authoring process. I feel that I've made this book exactly what it needs to be, and done it with a high-quality, attractive end result. If I've done my job, please rate, review, and tell others. And if not, by all means, first tell me what more I could add to make this book even better for you and others.

And, of course, information on typos & significant inaccuracies is always welcome for future editions (and others – it takes only a few moments to add a correction or a chapter that was overlooked).

Please email any and all feedback to **qr@eshlepper.com**. And of course, please take the time to **Review this book on Amazon.com.**

4. Introduction

QR Codes are simply everywhere, and despite frequent bashing by detractors, and a lull in the late twenty-teens that seemed to suggest their demise, they seem to be here to stay. Every once in a while, a technology or trend seems 'blessed from on high' and erupts on the scene with extreme popularity, for little or no reason. To be sure, QR Codes certainly have their many strengths and benefits, including unique benefits unachievable today by any other means; they are a great boon for advertising and marketing, particularly in the area of response tracking.

Surely, however, it seems that their ubiquity, their extreme popularity — certainly in 2012 when they seemingly reached their peak — is far out of proportion with their usefulness... since, since insofar as I am aware, they are used wrong most of the time, and never to the ultimate advantage — so in so very many cases, their usefulness is next to nil. Their widespread acceptance and employment has spread farther and faster than knowledge about how, why, where, and when to use them. They've simply been adopted, adored, and widely pressed into every manner of service.

Some uses are slick, well-conceived and skillful; but not many. By and large, most applications encountered are clumsy, ill-conceived, and leave the user, ie, the customer, prospect, or anyone scanning them (or attempting to scan) wondering: "What the heck?" This has left an impression with the public, from laypersons to professional marketers and bloggers, that QR Codes simply aren't useful. Rather, I would submit, since I've used them with great effect personally, and seen fantastic applications all over, they are simply not being utilized properly.

Why Are QR Codes Being Misused?

I attribute this misunderstanding primarily to the simple fact that QR Codes have erupted on the scene suddenly, and taken the world by storm. Their rise has been a grass-roots movement, with no authority in charge of the process, and it has spread haphazardly, as I will explain. In an instant, they leapt from total obscurity in tech-obsessed Japan, and are suddenly embraced all over. Anyone who can hold a sign, pass a business card, or place an advertisement is using QR Codes. You can't open a magazine, newsletter, newspaper, or pick up a product package or direct mail piece without seeing at least two or three, if not many more. The problem, I believe, is precisely this meteoric rise; their popularity has simply outstripped any attempt to document and define their use, enumerate *Best Practices*, explain what they're for, how to use them, and why.

Part of the reason for this chaotic state, as will be discussed later, is because DENSO WAVE INCORPORATED, originator of the QR Code, has declined to enforce its patent rights over the technology, essentially making QR Codes available to the world for free use. Without anyone actively controlling, monitoring, threatening, grousing, suing, asserting ownership claims, and quite notably, exclusively *monetizing* the technology, there is a near-vacuum of good, solid, authoritative information. To its credit, DENSO WAVE INCORPORATED has a great deal of information on QR Codes at their site. But, without formally asserting control, few have reason to refer to their site for guidance, or any reasonable likelihood of seeking out DENSO for information.

The creators of other technologies, who assert and protect their patent and copyrights more fully, have a greater impetus to promote the technology through richer documentation and implementation guides, and generally support their technologies to a fuller extent. Microsoft's Tag was an excellent example. And why not? They're making money off of it instead of just doing the world a favor.

Where is the Solid Information?

Not only that, but for entirely inexplicable reasons, the literature comes up short in hard facts; I've reviewed a number of titles in researching this book, surveying every title I could find, purchase, download, preview or browse, seeking to see how this topic has been handled in the literature; after all, I could hardly propose a project as ambitious as this one, without knowing that I had something substantial and valuable to contribute to the field. Indeed, I credit this book project to John T. Reed, who gives the following advice to authors: "If you don't have something significant to add to the topic, don't write a book" (my paraphrase).

Truly, I should have been able to easily find a resource that made this project superfluous. I'm still as surprised today that this project was necessary. And yet, without question, it was. Simply put, there weren't any, and certainly weren't any *good* options out there in the way of a well-assembled manual for how to get the best use and response from QR Codes.

I challenge anyone to find one. Even my usual favorite go-to publisher for nearly every purpose, the Wiley Publishing's "For Dummies®" series, left me with little more than a smattering of what QR Codes are. After a cover-to-cover reading, all I could ask was 'is that all?'

What's Been Done Already?

Don't get me wrong; there are many casual analyses out there about the concept of the QR Code, discussions of the novel math that formulates them, the coding & data storage scheme behind the QR Code, the potential capabilities of QR Codes, or expansive listings of the myriad applications for QR Codes. But, there is simply nothing in the way of a clear manual, spelling out a program for making the best use of them in marketing: The who, what, where, when, why and how of putting QR Codes to work for your enterprise.

If this isn't the first book on QR Codes you've purchased and read, you'll most certainly agree, because you've experienced first-hand the lack of practical information on applying QR Code technology to meet your marketing goals. You're not looking for a casual gloss of what a QR Code is. If you are looking for a quick gloss, then you are still reading the right book, as I've reviewed many titles and the first five or so chapters of this book do the same job that they do.

Who Is Writing These Books?

From appearances, it would seem that these books are written by authors who work in completely unrelated fields, but who have merely developed a passing curiosity with playing with QR Codes. Editing this edition in 2024 retrospectively, the wonder at the low quality is likely similar to what's found today with the proliferation of AI-generated content. Neither is a competent source for finding proven business uses. Nowhere have I found a broad and straightforward treatment of all areas of QR Code design, creation, implementation and use. So, as I've developed dozens of marketing campaigns utilizing QR Codes, I've kept meticulous notes on what I've learned, in the hope of creating a guide precisely like this one: full of useful and interesting information about QR Codes and their application in marketing, with real facts, proven techniques, and enough space to give their merit a full treatment; not to merely spit out a few quotable buzz-phrases and sound bytes; rather, to provide a solid, practical how-to of incorporating QR Codes into your current marketing today, and most importantly, to productive effect.

It's my hope that readers will be able to quickly understand what QR Codes are (and what they aren't), realize what they can add to their marketing efforts, and how to implement them to whatever degree they'd like; everything from simple tracking of scans and clicks, to full-featured and highly data-driven customer information captures, incorporating Landing Pages, online reporting, automatic responders, confirmation emails, Social Media integrations, and nearly every type of interaction that can be imagined.

And What of "Best Practices"?

In addition to the lack of "How-tos," there is correspondingly very, very little is being said about Best Practices, something I'll be exploring in detail. Every industry and process has professionals actively defining "Best Practices." Where are they on this topic? Clearly all too silent, or we wouldn't be subjected to a constant barrage of random QR Codes everywhere without a single explanation of their function or presence: As if they were readable by human eyes!

A sneak preview of one of my most important and most highly-recommended best practices:

Tell people what the heck it is, what to do with it, and why…

Or expect confusion, misapplication & failure.

There isn't enough information out there about how to apply them at all, let alone how to apply them in the best, most useful, productive, and successful ways. It seems that misunderstandings about what a QR Code is and shameful disregard for their proper context humbles marketing campaign after marketing campaign, and even leads some marketers to throw up their hands in defeat and concede that QR Codes just don't work.

Over the past several years, while I've been developing QR Code marketing concepts and strategies from numerous angles, I've read dozens of articles on the art or strategy of QR Code marketing. Alas, these articles invariably fall into one of several of the categories enumerated below:

- *Discussion of the underlying math & coding scheme.*
- *Bemused commentary about all the QR Codes everywhere.*
- *Grousing or Complaining about poor applications.*
- *Commentary about the QR Code fad*
- *Basic definitions of the QR Code, but little more.*
- *Pure sales material for a more expensive 2nd book purchase.*
- *Premature declarations of the QR Code's destiny of conquest.*
- *Premature declarations of the QR Code's humiliating end.*

Who This Book Is For?

If you're looking for so much more, including the real meat-and-bones of where those other books leave off, this book is the one that quickly glosses over where those end, and then proceeds to fill in all the real information that the others neglect to mention, or simply don't know for lack of practical experience. For you, the serious business-owner, online marketer, direct-mail or marketing professional, this is the guide that tells you what you need to know.

- *When should I include a QR Code?*
- *When should I not?*
- *What should I use my QR Code for?*
- *What should I not?*
- *Where should I put my QR Code for best effect & response?*
- *How do I place & promote my QR Code?*
- *Where would a QR Code be useless or unproductive?*
- *Where would a QR Code be downright silly and pointless?*
- *How do I get people to scan my QR Code?*
- *What are the obstacles to people responding?*
- *OK, enough talk! How do I do it?*
- *How do I track it?*
- *How do I make it great?*
- *How do I make it really, really, REALLY great, and do things never-before attempted? (one of my specialties)*

A Guide To The Perplexed

In the chapters that follow, all of these questions will be answered, to the fullest degree. By the end of the book, you'll be armed with the know-how to incorporate QR Codes into marketing programs of any size or scope, from single QR Codes for special functions, to hundreds of thousands of individually-coded and tracked QR Codes, standing ready to facilitate, monitor and report response from even the most massive direct-mail campaign or periodical publication. So, even if this isn't the first book on QR Codes that you've read, you can rest assured that it will be the last you'll ever need.

This Won't Be Painful

If I'm losing anyone already, don't worry. This isn't going to be painful. The boring and basic necessities will get glossed over very quickly (or reserved for later chapters, where they'll be essential); there are, after all, at least a dozen very nice titles that can do this mundane part admirably well. You won't need any knowledge of QR Codes or marketing principles to get everything you need out of this. I've included plenty of information and techniques for everyone, and worked hard to explain key terms as we go (and always remember that there is an extensive glossary at the end of the book, in case any of the terms do slip through without comment or footnote). So, don't be intimidated. This will start out simple, and will be easy to apply for everyone. It will get far more complicated and ambitious as the book progresses, in keeping with the promise of a comprehensive treatment of techniques — but that more advanced content is there for folks with that need. Everyone should be encouraged to stop reading when if feels like you have what you need, and anything more might be too much.

A Few Caveats

This title will boldly go where no one has gone before: Into the nitty-gritty how-to. It's not my desire that readers be left with a headache at the enormous complexity of the task ahead, and certainly not throw up their hands in frustration, assuming that they'll need a professional consultant to get the best there is from their marketing using QR Codes. Rather, my goal herein is to lay out tips, tricks and tools so that even the total layperson will be able to implement QR Codes into their Mobile Marketing campaigns competently and solidly, to great effect, and with any level of technical knowledge, including the absolute minimum level, *none.*

That being said, this book intends to give a full treatment of the entire concept and implementation of QR Code Mobile Marketing. As the chapters progress, there will be tools, concepts, and implementations presented that are beyond the average reader, and perhaps by rights should have been in another, more advanced title. At one point, they were included in two titles, precisely for this reason. The comments received were scathing: "Why do I have to buy two books?" "What a scam!" Consider it a free, additional bonus. Keep in mind that you're welcome to jump ship whenever you've had your fill. That's what's expected. You bought it, and you use it how you please. That's OK. You can put this book down whenever you want to. There's no shame in that. That's what I intended. Not everyone needs the more advanced techniques that I explore in the final chapters; most will never have a venue to need 20,000 or even one million uniquely-tracked QR Codes, self-host a friendly URL-shortening service, or some of the other final ideas outlined. Even the top professionals in the industry won't take advantage of more than 60% of these tactics in any single marketing campaign. The average reader will only need a quick understanding of some simple marketing techniques to understand what's possible, and how to implement them quickly, easily, productively and in all cases, *cheaply*.

The Ultimate Goal of QR Codes:

The single greatest strength, the sole reason for using QR Codes for marketing response is the ability of this technology to turn a simple printed object, whether a bumper sticker, a business card, or a sales display, into an internet-capable hyperlink for one-click access to nearly anything: a product purchase, contact information, videos, app download, etc. Remember that this is the point of everything that comes next: ***QR Codes act as a bridge between any printed page, and any digital media you can imagine.***

The Takeaway Message:

It's up to you. Take away from this book as little as you want, or as much as you need. Whether you just want to cut through the clamor of expensive online services offering to create a QR Code for you for $40-100, make a single QR Code for yourself, play with the various online demonstrations I've set up for personal fun and amusement, or even if you plan to integrate QR Codes into your business's marketing and direct response tracking on a massive and wildly ambitious level, everything you need is in here.

I'll try my best to make the journey as fun and interesting as possible – this isn't after-all intended to be a purely technical manual (perish the thought), but rather a practical guide to using QR Codes to useful effect for marketing, right now. Most users will have abandoned this book by then, and toddled off along their merry way with a few QR Codes and some great ideas, eager to put them to effective and profitable use.

Let's Begin with the Beginning.

In the meantime, let's start from the ground floor and work our way up. It would be inappropriate to begin a discussion of such an admittedly misunderstood technology anywhere but from the very beginning, bursting assumptions and correcting misconceptions as we go.

If you become bored over the next ten pages or so, please be comforted in the knowledge that your money was well spent… with any other title, those ten basic pages would be all you'd get... just dragged out interminably into a full book.

5. Why 2D Bar Codes?

Everywhere you look today, you see strange little black and white checkerboards. You can't get away from them. Clearly, you're very interested in what they're about, or you wouldn't be reading this book. The QR Code *Mobile Tagging* trend started a decade ago in tech-savvy Japan, trickled across Europe and now has hit American consumer markets. The chances are good that readers of this book are familiar with QR Codes, and have scanned them at some point.

But, the majority of people are probably left wondering, *"What are these QR codes? Why are they all over the place? What do they do? How do I use them?"* In this section, we'll explore the first question: What are they?

The 1-D Barcode

The QR Code is of course, in a nutshell, one of today's most modern and technologically advanced forms of a barcode. Below is a one-dimensional, or 1-D, barcode. A typical bar code is able to store anywhere from 5 or 6 digits, in the case of the typical retail store PLU, SKU or internal stock number, up to potentially 20 or so characters, such as the standard 13-Digit ISBN numbers (International Standard Book Numbers), the barcodes on the back of commercially-sold books (flip to the back cover for a great example). They've been in common use for decades, and automate digital input in many, many applications, mostly in retail and industrial settings.

A Typical 1-D Bar Code

Why Are "2-D" Barcodes Special?

In short, the answer is the quantity of data stored. A key drawback in a 1-D barcode is that the code is linear – it is in a single line or dimension, hence the designation '1-D'. As such, it must become longer and longer for every digit of data stored, as below. Thus, it quickly becomes too long to be scanned by nearly any typical barcode reader. After around 20 or so digits, the bar code simply becomes impossible to scan due to its length. The below simulated barcode gives an example of the upper limit of 1-D barcode technology.

PDF417 Code - With 13 unique data areas stacked, allowing many times more data than a 1-D code.

A 1-D Barcode far too long for any practical purpose.

Data Matrix Code

So, for data-intensive purposes, there have been several improvements made to the simple 1-D barcode, notably, the PDF-417 code, which stacks several 1-D bar codes, into a pseudo-2D bar code, with tracking and orientation bars at each side. As you can see from simply counting, the this PDF-417 code constitutes 13 separate barcodes, essentially stacked together, which are read separately by the bar code scanner, and combined together, allowing approximately 13 times more data.

After significant additional advances, we arrive at the Data Matrix code, which most closely resembles the QR Code, both in appearance as well as capabilities, with expandable modules (this one has four). It is basically only different in the lack of conspicuous alignment and orientation patterns. Of course, the specific underlying algorithms that encode the data vary greatly. In fact, of all the various 2D barcodes out there, the Data Matrix code is the only one that rivals the QR Code in terms of data storage capacity.

This Brings Us to The QR Code.

So, whereas a typical 1-D bar code can store fewer than 20 digits comfortably, such as the sample 1-D Barcode shown at the beginning of this chapter (from which data is read in the single dimension of the horizontal line), advanced 2D barcodes, such as the Data Matrix Code and the QR Code, can store hundreds or even thousands of characters. In fact, the QR Code has the capacity to store truly massive quantities of information, more than 7,000 total numeric characters, or 4,296 alphanumeric characters. This enables it to store website URLs of any conceivable length, to include tracking and meta-data information, appended data & query strings, which enable Smart Phones and other web-enabled mobile devices to decode them, use them to access web pages, and much more. So, their potential storage capacity is limitless, once paired with a portable scanner that is web-enabled, like any Smart Phone, a quick scan translates into a web address and is passed to the web browser; the QR Code can then take you anywhere, and trigger any number of online actions.

A Typical QR Code (2 Modules)

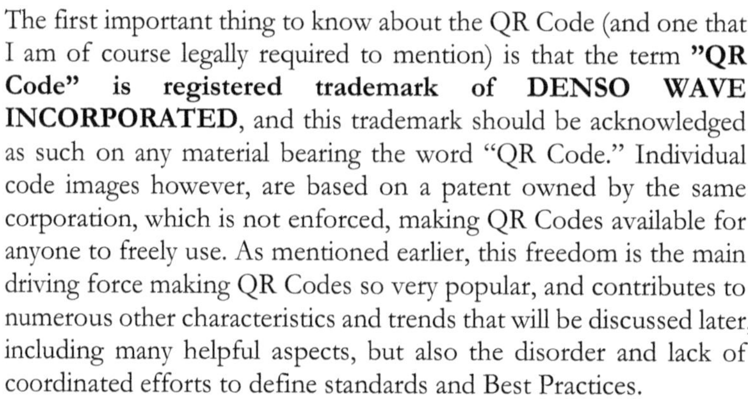

The first important thing to know about the QR Code (and one that I am of course legally required to mention) is that the term **"QR Code" is registered trademark of DENSO WAVE INCORPORATED**, and this trademark should be acknowledged as such on any material bearing the word "QR Code." Individual code images however, are based on a patent owned by the same corporation, which is not enforced, making QR Codes available for anyone to freely use. As mentioned earlier, this freedom is the main driving force making QR Codes so very popular, and contributes to numerous other characteristics and trends that will be discussed later, including many helpful aspects, but also the disorder and lack of coordinated efforts to define standards and Best Practices.

Some Brief, Boring Technical Stuff

I'll keep it brief. The technical standard that defines the QR Code is a protocol known as ***ISO 18004: QR Code 2005 Bar Code Specification***. ISO 18004 is an international standard of the International Standards Organization (ISO), an international regulatory body which documents accepted standards across hundreds of industries, including data exchange and transmission. Essentially, a QR Code is simply a bar code that conforms to a format defined by this international standard. Various documented standards include date & time formatting specifications (ISO-8601 and others), pressure-resistance for diving watches (ISO-8425), shatter-resistance for protective eyewear, the byte mapping for computer screen and print character sets (ISO-8859: the Latin alphabet and characters), various internet protocols, and durability and compatibility standards for hundreds of industries. One, among the thousands of these defined technical standards is ISO Standard number 18004, "QR Code 2005 Bar Code Specification," which defines the specification for formatting of QR Codes.

I admit it. I couldn't read or understand it. It's a pretty dry read, at a bit over 120 pages of exceedingly esoteric technical details and mathematics. It can be downloaded for a price of FS210 (210 Swiss Francs, perhaps US$300, depending on exchange rates, at *www.iso.org*. I certainly don't recommend actually doing this. But, it's up to you. Rarely is it valuable to understand how things work in order to be able to use them productively. The grunt work of generating QR Codes will always be done in an automated fashion, so the generator you use will handle the coding for you. There isn't much reason to understand the construction of a QR Code so deeply, unless you happen to be very ambitious and plan to create a QR Code generator yourself, from scratch. If so, you're reading the wrong book, because that's one of the few things beyond the scope of this book (although I've provided links in the index for several full-featured generator scripts that others have written, and can be freely downloaded to your website or embedded as you please).

It does bear mentioning that many firms that specialize in QR Code marketing frequently advertise that their QR Codes are ISO-18004 compliant, or are generated to the DENSO-WAVE specifications. I can't say how much of this is purely marketing fluff. But, it is worth noting that complex math goes into the QR Code encoding. You're really at the mercy of the programmer who creates the encoder. It's difficult to say whether the encoding is perfect, that is, "to spec" or simply "close enough." While anyone with the programming ability can read the specifications and write a program to encode data into a QR Code, this is certainly no guarantee that it was done entirely correctly. So, caveat emptor.

I have not, however, after scanning and generating thousands of QR Codes by hand as one-offs using every manner of service, as well as in bulk by the thousand, ever generated a QR Code that did not scan flawlessly (except when the reason was quite evident). So, either everyone is doing it perfectly, or it's not all that difficult. And even today, after *yet another* ten years of generating QR Codes, I have yet to find a generator that didn't work as advertised.

Still, I have noticed that varied encoders will almost always produce dramatically different *looking* QR Codes, given the exact same data. Further, some encoders default to certain version numbers, etc. So, testing with multiple scan applications is always a must. You never know when you might find an encoder that's a lemon.

That's All the Boring Stuff

I'm through. It had to be mentioned, and for that I apologize. All you'll get is three pages of that from me. Most descriptions of QR Code functionality dwell too long on the technical specifications of the data coding, which is really all that you'd get from a deep reading of the ISO specification. And yet, that's what many writers do in speaking about QR Codes; that's a big mistake. The data coding scheme is just a means to an end, and really should be paid little attention, by and large.

The sole exception to this ignoring of the technical aspects is when you need to understand a few of the technical limitations that need to be communicated in order for QR Codes to function properly. These will all be discussed in later chapters, for purely practical purposes, in ensuring that you don't break your new QR Codes. Yes, we're going to break a few along the way as well, but it's all for a good cause. Once we finish, I assure you, you'll be thoroughly convinced of the value of breaking your own QR Codes too, on occasion.

But For Now, Forget the Structure!

Nobody contemplates the stoichiometric ratios in their car's engine that support the balanced chemical reactions and clean combustion; Seriously? Instead, we turn down the top, turn up the radio, and cruise, right? That's what we're here to do with QR Codes. The most important point to communicate is not the structure and data coding scheme of the QR Code, but rather the multimedia functionality that they enable. Forget the how. It's all about the *"what"*. If you can do it on the web with a web browser, you can do it with a quick snap of a QR Code. The entire Internet is instantly at the fingertips of any customer with a Smart Phone. Uses include:

- *Dialing a phone number.*
- *Sending an Email (even one pre-populated with subject and body).*
- *Preparing an SMS (text) message (with recipient & text).*
- *Displaying miscellaneous text messages*
- *Opening an app on your device.*
- *Triggering a script or 'Webhook'.*
- *Directing to any web page (Landing Pages, Application downloads, restaurant menus, Videos, eCommerce Check-Out pages, etc)*
- *Deep-linking to a long-tailed, dynamic, or machine-generated URL that would be impossible for mere mortal to type by hand (let alone on a mobile device)*
- *Downloading VCard or MeCard info.*
- *Sending nearly unlimited data & information along with the scan.*
- *Directing to a web form for registrations, entries, requests.*
- *Confirming receipt of items and documents.*
- *Displaying a Map or directions to any location.*

- *Literally dozens of other basic, core functions, with hundreds of applications*
- *Error-proofing interactions to prevent consumers from being mis-directed, or mis-keying information.*
- *Quickly swapping devices to continue a web visit on a different device – without exchanging any information except optically.*
- *Syncing information between devices without exchanging data (secure applications like Whatsapp and TFA Authentication devices/apps).*

2-D Barcodes in Today's World

Today, these barcodes serve the same purpose that they always have: they provide accurate, fast, automated access to data. Just as the barcode scanners at the checkout of your local grocery store, highway tollbooth, or department store add speed, accuracy, and automation to the purchase process, these are the same strengths that QR Codes and other advanced barcode systems harness to automate everyone's favorite leisure activity… web-surfing from our Smart Phones. And that's no joke. Mobile browsing, shopping, and gaming are growing far faster than other Internet traffic usage. QR Codes make accessing information fast, accurate, and infinitely more engaging, interesting, rich, and versatile. They are barcodes… with a twist: they don't speed up mundane and disinteresting activities like paying for groceries; rather, they facilitate our play, socializing, and entertainment in ways unlike any other tool.

A Quick Self-Check:

But, before we get to actually creating QR Codes it's important to remember, just as with most marketing efforts, and the tools used in consumer circles: this is one of those technologies that everyone seems to be pouncing on, just because. Many, many marketers and business owners haven't stopped to ask themselves, *"is this something that is needed, desirable, and productive for my business?"* I would say that the answer is "ABSOLUTELY." But, how to employ them truly depends on what you'd like to get done. And the skill behind the implementation will determine how well that gets done.

6. Who Uses QR Codes?

A quick survey of popular online literature, technology, marketing and business Blogs, magazine articles, trade publications, newspapers, etc, will reveal that the value of QR Codes for marketing is usually a foregone conclusion to most commentators and bloggers: they already know what the right answer is, whether yeah or nay. A quick survey of opinions reveals opinions ranging from ecstatic cheerleading about their stellar future, to announcements that they're a dead technology, and hailing their replacements (and this is potentially from the same Blogger on the same day).

But, What are the Real Facts?

There are many, many examples published and referenced all over the Internet that claim to demonstrate the abject failure of QR Codes. For example, in researching this book, I reviewed the findings of a survey conducted by the "Youth Marketing" firm *Archrival.* This report article stated that in a survey of 500 students across 24 college campuses, it was revealed that this demographic was not likely to scan QR codes. What they reported was the following:

- *81% of students reported that they owned a Smart Phone.*
- *80% of students reported previously having seen a QR Code.*
- *21% of students successfully scanned the QR code provided.*
- *75% of students reported that they are "Not Likely" to scan a QR code in the future.*

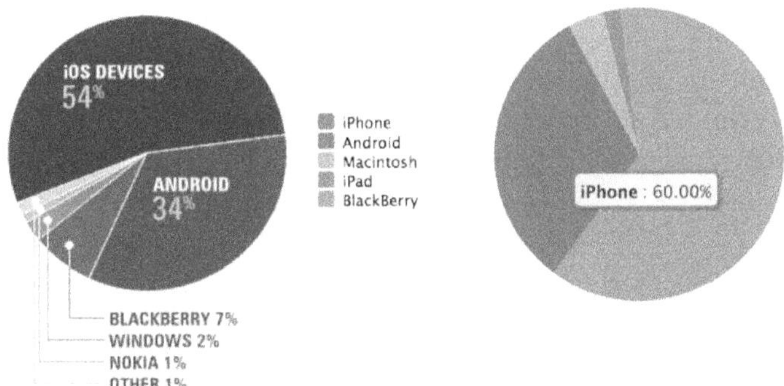

Mobile OS QR Code scan usage recorded by QRStuff.com, from their 2011 QR Code Creation & Data Usage Trends Report. © 2011-2012 QRStuff.com

Sample data from a single, live QR Code-driven Mobile Marketing campaign conducted by the author. © 2013 Daniel Benjamin

Professional, Real-World Experience

I'm not sure how precisely these results were generated, since I can say for certain that these results, as generated for this demographic do not translate into results for the ones with which I've dealt. I do have a number of ideas about why these results may have been so abysmal. My best guess is that self-report is a notoriously difficult experimental technique really only useful in gauging what consumers think about themselves. As in most things, what people think and say, and what they actually do are usually two completely different things.

Quite to the contrary, the consumer response to QR Codes in marketing materials I've generated has been stellar, in my own humble opinion. My own experience with QR codes, not in a single, purely hypothetical, question and answer session, but rather in live, active, successful, revenue-producing, real-world, professionally-run marketing campaigns is just the opposite. Response is great.

Here is sample data documenting a bit of the information immediately available from a Mobile Marketing campaign utilizing QR Codes, showing the demographics of the devices used to scan the codes. The takeaway message? Consistent, comparable response and usage data across multiple long-term campaigns show that QR Codes are in use, not merely being generated, but being actively scanned by consumers, by the million.

QR Code Results

In my own experience, when a QR Code was added to supplement a URL or PURL, Overall click-through response (Landing Page visitors) increased by 35%, due to the ease with which consumers could access the Landing Page (no need to hunt & peck at a tiny smartphone screen; rather, they access it with a single snap).

Of total Landing Page visitors, 50-60% of the new total arrived via QR Code Scan. (indicating that the responders asserted a definite preference for QR Code response – the additional visitors (that 35%) would only respond via QR Code, and many who might have responded otherwise chose to scan instead.

On the destination page, form completions jumped as compared to abandonments (owing to the unique ability of QR Codes to store and pass on data to the Landing Page, making data entry easier for the visitor, universally a mobile device user)

Why Is This?

Some conclusions as to why this is the trend:

- *Nearly 1/3 of potential respondents wouldn't bother typing the URL, and would only respond through the QR Code Scan; their response is entirely due to the QR Code's presence, and they would not respond otherwise.*
- *Another 1/3 of respondents will respond via a URL, but still actively choose to respond via the QR Code, for convenience.*
- *Pre-populating form data via supplemental data hidden in the QR Code data through some means (encoding, URL-shortening, or server-side programming) made the forms faster and easier to complete, and thus more user-friendly, promoting form completions and data capture that wouldn't be possible in any other way.*

In some consumer response and research and testing conducted by my company, I've observed some impressive trends in QR code scans.

- *In test campaigns, when recipients are offered QR code scans in addition to any other means of online response, including standard URLs& PURLs, they chose the QR Code scan as the top response method.*
- *That's a net 30% increase in (landing page) response over similar campaigns without the QR codes.*
- *Of those responses, 60% were through the QR codes, indicating that tech-savvy consumers (ie, internet and Smart Phone users) prefer QR codes for responding to offers by a margin of nearly 3:2.*
- *Thus, adding a QR Code to a campaign can add 35% additional response, as well as shifting response from other means as consumers assert their preference for QR Code scans.*

Some Other Perspectives

Now, as much as I believe that my own personal experience should be considered entirely convincing, persuasive and authoritative for all, that's all purely anecdotal. For anyone else not blessed to live inside my beautiful and infallible brain, a broader and more proven picture is certainly preferable. What are the captains of the QR Code industry saying about QR Code scans? Publishers of mobile barcode scanning applications, and the top barcode generation utilities are uniquely positioned to give us the best possible glimpse into precisely how many people are scanning, and how they are scanning. After all, they are able to record each and every scan made using their software, and quantify it all for investigation. Here's what they have to say on the subject.

Scanbuy *(www.ScanLife.com)* published research on mobile barcode scans recorded using its ScanLife Smart Phone application, one of the top QR Code scanning applications, and one of my own recommended apps. Scanbuy manages mobile campaigns for many national brands and recognizable names. In just the first three months of 2013, Scanlife reported more than 18 million scans, with 6.7 million in the month of March alone. Not surprising, in a trend dating back to 2009 when reporting started, QR Code scanning continues to grow, and March 2013 (the most recent month of the most recent quarter reported) is the single highest month in history for QR Code scans, with the United States leading the world in QR Code scans with ScanLife's app.[1] That's not 18 million QR Code scans worldwide… that's 18 million for this one single app publisher among hundreds or thousands. Keep that in mind as you read on.

3GVision, *(www.i-Nigma.com)* publisher of the iNigma QR Code reader, my own #1 recommended app, whose enterprise clients for hosted solutions include FHM Magazine, Cosmopolitan, The Sun, as well as tech giants Sanyo, Kyocera, Motorola, Nokia, NEC, Toshiba, Hitachi, Samsung, Sharp, LG, Sony Ericsson & Casio, has reported 20%+ yearly global growth in bar code scans, since the 2009 reporting year, with 35.1% growth for Canada, 42.1% year-over-year growth for the United States, and even higher growth for other countries. Usage is massively on the rise.

QRStuff, *(www.QRStuff.com)*, a QR Code generation site, noted that global QR Code generation increased 315% during 2011 to 2.7 million codes generated,[2] and global QR Code scanning increased by 862% (992% for the United States alone). They also recorded scan activity in 58 new nations not seen previously in scan activity, bringing the total to 200 countries engaged, worldwide. Once again, 2.7 million for one single web service generating QR Codes among thousands.

Pitney Bowes, *(www.pb.com)* the mailing, postage and print industry leader, concludes their 2012 *White Paper on the emerging QR Code marketing trend* indicating that 27% of adults age 18-34 in the US, UK, France & Germany, actively interact with QR Codes, and lists the top locations where consumers scan QR Codes as (in descending order of frequency) magazines, direct mail, product packaging & posters, online, among other locations. Still, Pitney Bowes carefully notes that the QR Code is *only* in its infancy. In other words, the triple-digit growth observed here and elsewhere in QR Code use is only the beginning.

Why is This Just the Beginning?

First and foremost, to ram this point home again, these figures represent only a tiny glimpse at a scant few individual source sites for generating and scanning QR Codes, among dozens of major sites and services, hundreds of minor ones, and infinite thousands of independent scripts, plugins, and installations. The potential total number is simply staggering. Behind that, there is a number of reasons for this growth and usage:

First and foremost, they're Fast. Simply put, QR Codes enable a 'Quick Response[3],' turning a single touch of a phone key into a webpage, or nearly anything imaginable, without so much as having to type a single character. The response is fast, and the content delivered is faster. It's available instantly, on demand, just like today's consumers want, and to which they have become accustomed.

Second, they're immediate: Latency is a serious problem for marketers, and refers to the delay between encountering a marketing message and actually responding to it. The more immediately a prospect can respond, the greater the likelihood that they will, in fact, respond. Conversely, the longer it takes for them to respond, the less likely they are to respond. It doesn't take a PhD in psychology to understand why. Simple procrastination and forgetfulness mean that many marketing messages are simply forgotten, since they didn't meet with instant action. A consumer may not sit down at home in front of a desktop system for perhaps hours, days, the weekend, or ever again. By the time they do, are they going to remember your Landing Page, website, or offer at all? Not likely. At best, if the offer happens to be one that really appealed to them, they'll at some point recall the offer and have no idea how to access it, giving up... or perhaps finding it... or the website of a better-positioned competitor. You get the idea.

However, a consumer's phone is always with them, always turned on and always ready-to-go. Using a mobile device has long since become the preferred way of browsing the Internet for more and more consumers every day. With a QR Code, they can strike while the iron is hot, where they are, when they see your offer, instantly.

It's Easier. When all other factors are equal, fast and easy wins out, hands down. Taking the easy road is simply better. Who doesn't prefer the path of least resistance? I know I do, and so do all consumers. Keep in mind that at home, users will type on large, comfortable keyboards. But, while out and about, their miniscule smart phone keyboards are all they have. So, they will always prefer any shortcut around typing or texting on them. True, texting gets easier and easier as Smart Phones evolve. There was T9 predictive text, then there were QWERTY, slide-out keyboards, and then touch screens with soft keyboards, advanced predictive text input & auto-correction, voice recognition, and even mobile Social Media logins that will automatically log in a user from stored account data in their device.

Still, the size of screens and keyboards will always be at odds with basic phone portability: Everyone wants a larger screen or keyboard, but nobody wants a larger, heavier phone. So, nobody will ever get a *far* larger keyboard to use, just variations of the same general size. A quick scan of a QR Code will always be easier.

It's interesting and trendy. I'm not a gadget guy, nor one to follow the crowd and chase the next-best-biggest-baddest-better-deal. But, for all the reasons above, and some purely fortunate reasons, people like to scan QR Codes. They do. But more importantly, QR Codes have gained widespread acceptance by the public as a de-facto standard for responding to offers and accessing online content. There is the physical address to visit, the phone number to dial, the email address to send, and the website or Landing Page to visit, but the fastest, easiest, and most error-proof way possible to visit the website or Landing Page is with a QR Code scan.

Regarding Smart Phones

Oh, and by the way… Incidentally, that small, hand-held device that your online visitor pecks at incessantly during dinner, dates, work, movies, and loves enough to bejewel, bedazzle, decoupage, accessorize, and outfit with a $50 case custom printed with a photograph of their children? Well, I'll have you know that it just happens to be all of the following (in case you forgot):

- *A phone that can instantly dial your sales number.*
- *A phone that can instantly send a text (even pre-written)*
- *A device to display a map and directions to your location.*
- *A computer to email in response to your offer, even pre-written.*

- *A web browser, ready to visit and display your website or Landing Page.*
- *A portable media player delivering amusing, useful, or interesting videos or media that you might recommend on command, right now.*
- *A QR Code scanner to instantly serve up any of these with a single touch.*

Opportunities for engagement like *that* make QR Codes precisely an avenue you'll want to pursue for your marketing.

Enter Mobile Marketing

The broad, all-encompassing term for all aspects of meeting customers on their terms: the mobile devices they love, have on their persons always, and in most cases prefer for all their online interactions, communications, tasks, chores, activities, education, amusements, and entertainment. In short, the Smart Phone is the perfect multi-channel response device, for any product or service you plan to sell or promote... hence, the term trending in the business world, "Mobile Marketing." The Smart Phone screen has been dubbed the "Third Screen": the third new "screen" in our lives after the TV and computer.

Now, this book's thrust is most specifically geared toward the application of QR Codes to meet your Mobile Marketing needs, a topic that requires at least a book-length treatment all its own. It's not the intent of this book to fully develop the concept of Mobile Marketing, but rather to presume it, and focus on how to use QR Codes as a response medium. But ultimately, no discussion of QR Codes can be started without simultaneously addressing Mobile Marketing, for one diabolically obvious reason:

QR Codes Are For Mobile Devices

Just in case you didn't realize this. Exclusively, and without exception, QR Codes are for Mobile Devices alone. No QR Code has ever been scanned from a desktop computer.[4] All QR Code scanners are applications loaded onto mobile devices & Smart Phones. iPods? Yes. Smart Phones? Yes. Desktop computers? Not a chance. Never. QR Codes are the grease that can open up Mobile Marketing of every sort and type, for faster and easier response, better user experience, higher response, and in general the best and highest use of your marketing effort and dollars.

But, it is vital that it be understood that while mobile device users are a rich market and a massive demographic, they have many special needs that cannot be ignored if Mobile Marketing is to be a success. It is for this reason that Mobile Marketing is often discussed independently from other more general aspects of marketing. It's also for this reason that much will be written about Mobile Marketing concepts, practices, and strategies herein, all along the way.

A Breather to Get Things Straight

Exciting, I know. But, before you skip the next three chapters, race through producing a QR Code, run out to your local print shop, get some QR Codes printed up and slap one on everything you see, there's far more that you need to consider.

Unfortunately, it does seem that this is precisely what is being done by far too many businesses to count, judging from the QR Codes that we see everywhere, including billboards, business cards, roadside signs, and even 'kinetic outdoor marketing' (people standing by the roadside twirling signs), T-shirts, coffee mugs, and every conceivable type of media.

QR Codes are definitely trendy right now, as you already know, or else you'd never be reading these pages. But, following a trend without understanding it or knowing how to make the most of it is simply foolish.

The perceived legitimacy, versatility, and utility of QR Codes has been very much damaged by ill-conceived applications, including outright misuse of QR Codes. Before risking further muddying the waters by adding another confusing and poorly-executed QR Code to the trash heap, possibly resulting in an another annoyed Blog article decrying the "*Untimely Demise of the QR Code*," carefully consider the following:

Always Address Function First

When something is trendy, it's in-demand, über-hot, and everybody feels they need to have one; or two; or seven adorable ones in every color of the rainbow, each with cute embroidered labels for every day of the week, because they'll look so precious sporting them around. To be sure: QR Codes *are* cool. And interesting. But, they're not just pop-art icons, nor merely for decoration, although that may come as shocking news to many out there.

They certainly can be made to be quite decorative, and later chapters will cover just how to go about making them so. But, QR Codes are not mere decoration, and treating them as such without any concept as to what they can bring to the table functionally is to devalue them and set oneself up for disappointment. They are a tool for marketing and direct response, a functional, interactive part of your online presence and your Mobile Marketing plans that requires understanding, planning, and implementation. It isn't necessarily difficult, complicated, expensive, or complex. In fact, a simple critical reading of this book will equip you with everything you need to sidestep the biggest problems altogether, and get the job done right, at any level of the game.

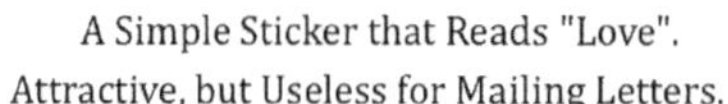
A Simple Sticker that Reads "Love". Attractive, but Useless for Mailing Letters.

An Actual Postage Stamp Valid for Mailing Services with the USPS.

An Apt Analogy

But, treating QR Codes like high-tech decoration and jumping into QR Code printing and production with both feet, fully embracing it in ignorance, only to emblazon everything with QR Codes, absent any rhyme, reason, or sense, is much akin to putting random decorative stickers on the corners of envelopes you plan to mail, simply because everyone else you see is putting cute little heart-shaped stickers on the corner of their letters, too; if you don't realize that postage stamps are something quite unique, a very special type of sticker, your letters won't get there. Never in a million years. It may look like a letter, it may walk like a letter, and it may even quack like a letter. But, it's a no-go situation: it will never get your message to its intended destination. Ever.

Postage stamps mean something, represent something, and do something very specific. They allow the letter to make it through the mail, contingent on rules, guidelines, reams of postal regulations, placement, value, weight limits, and dozens of other conditions and concerns. To ignore any of these is to court disaster: returned letters, lost letters, wasted time, money, printing cost, etc.

A QR Code Isn't a Magic Charm or Emblem

Similarly, a QR Code has functions, features, and rules that govern its use in the most quantifiable way. These will be discussed at length in the later chapters. They are a tool to use for its intended purpose, and consistent with proven, sensible principles for best use. To do otherwise is to sabotage your intended purpose. If there's no intended purpose, don't be terribly surprised if no magical results proceed from displaying it. A QR Code isn't, after all, some magical charm or totem that confers a mystical blessing to your business. In other words, a hammer has a use. When you need one, it makes quick work of the job. But there is no substitute when you need a hammer: a screwdriver, blow-torch or caulk gun simply will not do. Proudly displaying one on the wall of your office isn't likely to do any good whatsoever. Unless it happens to be a magic hammer, in which case, hold on tight, click your heels and make a wish.

The Implementation Game Plan

The best first step is to take some time to consider just what a QR Code is, what it is not, and what it can do for your marketing efforts, both in print, online, and everywhere, in relation to mobile marketing response and response tracking (just some cold water thrown in the faces of the doting masses and gloomy naysayers alike). That's the goal of the next chapter. The takeaway message here: Function over Form. If you don't have a purpose for a QR Code, you don't need one yet. And, before you know if you need one, you'll need to understand what QR Codes are for, and what's possible with them. Then you'll be able to see what they can do for you. But before we get too deep into the lessons, we're going to take a quick break to make a few QR Codes, just for the heck of it.

---

[1] *Bear in mind that the QR Code scan totals for Scanbuy, as well as all the others listed only reflect a single application & Landing Page service vendor. There are literally hundreds of scan applications, including those listed in the next chapters. So, if 6.7 million scans in March isn't impressive enough, just bear in mind that this is one application among hundreds.*

[2] *Actual global QR Code generation and scanning volume is potentially hundreds of times larger. QRStuff.com, of course, despite my own personal affection for it, is just one site among many thousands that generate QR Codes.*

[3] *"QR" is not an acronym for Quick Response, despite the popularity of that explanation. DENSO-WAVE holds patents on the QS and QT codes as well, and many other Q-codes. QR is just another in the series. Remember, DENSO-WAVE designed these not for marketing response, but for internal factory uses. The acronym is false.*

[4] *Actually, it is possible to scan a QR Code from a desktop computer. The best way I've found for the sake of troubleshooting a QR Code perhaps, is to visit Zebra Crossing's website and use their QR Code decoder, which allows an image upload and decodes from the image. Visit http://code.google.com/p/zxing for many useful tools, including a QR Code decoder that allows QR Code image uploads for processing.*

7. Setting Up Shop

Before we get too far along on this journey, it's assumed that you're going to be generating and scanning QR Codes. So, at the very minimum, you'll need a QR Code scanner for your Smart Phone, and access to the Internet to use an online QR Code generator. There are hundreds, if not thousands of web services, utilities, and applications available to generate and scan QR Codes. There are even Smart Phone application QR Code scanners that can create their own QR Codes on the mobile device. But even in that case, you'll need to put them somewhere else to scan them. Before you get started working on a few QR Codes, it's important to keep a few things in mind.

A Hundred Ways to Skin a Cat

As mentioned earlier, DENSO WAVE INCORPORATED doesn't enforce its patent rights over the QR Code data-coding scheme. The data storage scheme is available to the public via the ISO documents. What that means is that anyone with programming expertise can simply read the manual, program an application to encode QR Codes according to the standard, and churn out QR Codes by the billion

There are literally a million sources of QR Codes, ranging from the simplest and most basic QR Codes from an address-bar API (Application Programming Interface) call to the most beautiful and dramatic QR Codes that incorporate color gradients and even miniature logos, up to and including one-off custom artistic creations that meld images into QR Codes and are truly artistic. Each has its place.

But, it's important to remember when starting to experiment that the QR Code standard (ie, the underlying coding that creates it) is public, and has been extensively developed by thousands of application developers and web programmers. So, try not to fall into the trap of *paying* for QR Codes. As a professional marketer who makes a living in QR Codes and Mobile Marketing, this is a shocking thing to write. But in all honesty, there are simply too many amazing free services out there offering free QR Code generation. There's no reason to start paying for QR Codes. They can be made anywhere for free. So, despite the mystique that you may feel about this technology, you won't need programming knowledge for web or mobile application development to put QR Codes to great use for your business today, and you certainly don't need to shell out loads of cash to pay anyone for QR Code generation.

The 21 Keystroke QR Code

Case in point: The simplest way in the universe to generate a QR Code is to simply tell Google to make one for you. Type the following into your internet browser's address bar, and Google will instantly display a QR Code image for whatever URL you specify to create a QR Code containing anything you place after the equal sign[1].

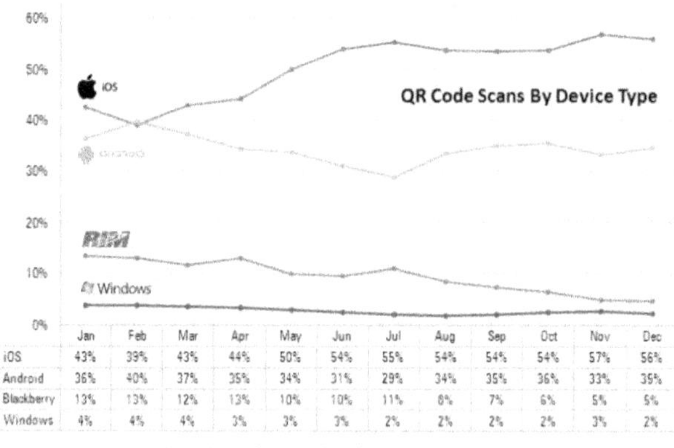

	Jan	Feb	Mar	Apr	May	Jun	Jul	Aug	Sep	Oct	Nov	Dec
iOS	43%	39%	43%	44%	50%	54%	55%	54%	54%	54%	57%	56%
Android	36%	40%	37%	35%	34%	31%	29%	34%	35%	36%	33%	35%
Blackberry	13%	13%	12%	13%	10%	10%	11%	8%	7%	6%	5%	5%
Windows	4%	4%	4%	3%	3%	3%	2%	2%	2%	2%	3%	2%

2011 QR Code Creation & Data Usage Trends Report
QRStuff.com | www.QRStuff.com ©2011-2012

```
https://chart.googleapis.com/chart?cht=qr&chs
=150x150&chl=Hi
```

See. QR Codes aren't magical or mystical. Anyone can pull them out of thin air just by just asking.

Just the Bear Necessities

Now, there are astonishingly fancy options out there, and I promise that I'll get to that in time. In later chapters, we'll touch on some of the more involved and fancier QR Code generation tools, and custom options to make a professional impression in style. I *promise.* But, for now it's sufficient to get started simply and get some great-functioning QR Codes under your belt! And to do so, you'll need some basic equipment. You'll most certainly need the following:

- *Access to the internet*
- *An online QR Code generator*
- *A Smart Phone capable of Scanning QR Codes, with either the Android, Blackberry, Windows Mobile, or iOS.*
- *A QR Code Scanning App Installed on your phone*

If you don't have a Smart Phone or other mobile device with a camera, and internet access, then I'm very sorry, but our relationship is about to come to an abrupt end: They're completely necessary in order to create, scan and trouble-shoot QR Codes. The rest, you can get online.

Other Devices are certainly possible and have much support for QR Code scanning, but Android OS Phones & iOS (iPhones, iPods & iPads) are the top devices used to scan, based on the results of every campaign I've run, as well as the data published by others in the marketing industry, to include QrStuff.com and others. The breakdown is roughly 60/40 one way or the other, sometimes with some single-digit percentages coming from other phone operation systems, notably Blackberry/RIM and Windows Mobile OS phones.

I blame low market saturation for these two underdogs; Android & iPhone are simply the overwhelmingly dominant leaders. See:

Getting Started Creating QR Codes

In order to get started creating a few QR Codes, you're going to need access to a few key applications to create & test your new QR Codes. There are hundreds, if not thousands of online services available for this. Below is a smattering of some simple ones that are great for a beginner to play with. In fact, I've selected these specially because they are simple… so that you won't get distracted and off task. See the appendix later for the exhaustive list of recommended sites. Each has its relative merits and capabilities, and I'll make use of each liberally in many of the examples that follow in later chapters.

Recommended Basic Generators

Many, many more will come later, but for now, you just need one, and a simple one that won't cause too many distractions.

- *http://www.GoQr.com - Simple and bare bones. Recommended.*
- *http://www.QrStuff.com - A bit much for beginners – but my top favorite; If you'd like to get started using it now, I'll tolerate the small distraction.*[2]

Recommended QR Code Scanning Apps:

And of course, since the QR Code is a two-way street, you're going to need a mobile device to scan them; I am going to have to assume that you have your own mobile device to which you are rather partial, and have access to for scanning. Fair warning: your choices may be limited if you're not using an Android or iOS device.

iNigma – My favorite, and billed as the world's most popular QR Code scanner. Fast & Simple. Although I have literally a dozen QR Code readers installed on my Smart Phone, iNigma has become the single, first and best go-to reader for my every need. Why? It scans fast, accurately, and most of all, reliably. iNigma scans everything I throw at it without complaint, problem, or delay. Performs well, even when reading QR Codes from computer monitors, or in lower contrast. For actual scans, I recommend it highly[3].

Microsoft's TAG reader, a version that supports both QR Code and Tag scans.[4] As loathe as I am to give credit to Microsoft, I have to give them their due. Their app is excellent, as is the Tag and the their commitment to support QR Code scans with their application (as we'll discuss later). Further, their documentation, white papers and fact-sheets about QR Code/Tag implementation is outstanding.

Figure 1 Customized Code

An example of customizable options (in this case, a logotype inserted) into the QR Code matrix.

QR+ -- And interesting app, with a number of excellent features. Save a QR Code for later use, process a scan from an existing photo on your device, and even enables creation of QR Codes directly within the App… with custom text and color overlays (such as this one[5]), and even more in the paid version of the app. That being said, since the process is fully automated, the text that it inserts is done in the most clumsy way possible, such that the resulting QR Code has a huge data load, and is difficult to read. Unique features found nowhere else. Good choice. Don't actually use it to create QR Codes with words overlaid.

NeoReader – Also fast & Simple. Has given me some difficulties when it comes to scanning some designer codes, and any directly from a computer screen (which, unfortunately is the first stage of testing, before printing proof copies). It may also have some difficulty with colored codes or lower contrast. It also has had difficulty with several designer QR Codes that were easily scanned by other readers.

Red Laser – Good features, but not as easy-to-use as iNigma & NeoReader. Also, not a dedicated QR Code reader, with some 1-D barcode scan capabilities. Generally solid performance without trouble.

ScanLife – Another solid performer, that works quite well. In addition to their reader, ScanLife does a great deal of enterprise Landing Page hosting, as well.

Revisiting this library of scanning apps in 2024, how times have changed! On-board camera apps now automatically recognize QR Codes, particularly for iOS and Android device users, making the scanning process seamless. This seamless integration without need for directing less tech-savvy consumers to an appropriate app for downloading *dramatically* enhances the consumer experience and adoption. Still, for special purposes (decoding, troubleshooting, maintaining scan history, etc, a dedicated app is essential). As previously noted, iNigma is always the recommendation.

So, that's the end of the chapter. Before proceeding on, Kindly visit your phone OS's application store, or consult your on-device app library, and download a scanner app. It will be needed shortly. Please use I-Nigma. Thanks.

---

[1] *The Google Charts API is extremely useful for various purposes, QR Codes being one of the less interesting, as a matter of fact; feel free to explore it some more and I'm sure you'll agree. Visit the charts API sandbox, where you can explore hundreds of varieties of amazing infographics that can be generated based on your data in moments, even programmatically from your website. For the sake of simplicity, I shortened the URL to make it easier to type and keep the focus of the demonstration on creating a QR Code, and skip explaining the underlying complete API call, which can be found in the Google Charts API Documention (see references).*

[2] *QRStuff.com has a full-featured QR Code & Shortlink management system that is top-notch. Before starting your production QR Codes, be sure to get an account, so that all your QR Codes & Short Links can be archived permanently. Any you create from the homepage may be lost to you forever.*

[3] *However, and this cannot be overemphasized, for testing one's own QR Codes, i-Nigma may be too reliable. After all, it cannot be assumed that the scanning public will have the best reader. More*

likely, they will have an average reader. So, for testing purposes, another will be preferred. Many of my more exotic, hand-edited designer QR Codes scan instantly with i-Nigma, while other scanner apps can't get it right.

[4] *More information on the Microsoft Tag can be found in Chapter 16, QR Code Competitors.*

[5] *However, I certainly don't recommend doing it this way. It's somewhat clumsy, and can be done much better with an overlay in any image editor, simply by upping error correction. See Chapter 11, Bending the Rules for more on logo overlays.*

8. Your Second QR Code

If you used the Google API example in the foregoing chapter, this may already be your second QR Code; if you're not so daring, we'll call it your first. Moving forward, it's going to be assumed that you've read the foregoing chapters and have followed the instructions, downloading a QR Code scanning app from your Smart Phone's app library or store, and browsed a few of the online QR Code generators provided. If you've found one that you're happy with, by all means stick with it... it's probably more than adequate, you already know how to use it, and you're good to go. As we progress into later chapters, you'll develop a more substantial idea of just how you're going to use the QR Codes, as well as the related technologies that are applied with them, and you'll be able to judge best whether the generator you've chosen meets your needs or needs to be replaced.

Now, To Create A QR Code...

- *1. Choose a URL for which you'd like to generate a QR Code.*
- *2. Visit your chosen QR Code generator website.*
- *3. Type in the URL and click 'Create QR Code' (or whatever)*
- *4. Download the QR Code image file & give it a descriptive name.*
- *5. Print your QR Code (or first put it on your document)*
- *6. Scan the QR Code with your Smart Phone's scanner app.*

Voilá! A QR Code

Pat yourself on the back! That's the whole job. Well, not quite. There are a few things to consider. In truth, you've just accomplished only the simplest mechanics of generating a QR Code. Unfortunately, for most, this is where the process ends. This isn't so terribly surprising, since this is where the process seems to end in most of the literature available on QR Codes, including the "*QR Codes for the Total and Utter Moron*" book. Why would any individual QR Code user do anything further with the technology, when the experts seem to believe that this is where the game ends? Or at least this is all that's possible to expect of the lay reader.

Where to Stick It...

So, in every other book, this is the end. All you get is a QR Code and a list of places to stick it. Well, this book isn't about taking a few dollars of your money, just to tell you where to stick it, and it's not about leaving off where the others do. It's about picking up where they left off. So, here we go...

9. Why Use QR Codes?

A long-time associate of mine, who runs a direct mail company, maintains a file of useful and interesting mailers and other marketing materials that he's come across over the years, both good and embarrassingly, abysmally bad. This is really common practice in most creative industries, and is called a "swipe file," for obvious reason: they're ideas and concepts that catch one's eye, and that one may wish to swipe in the future. That's not a bad thing. There are rarely any truly new ideas out there: usually, only evolutionary changes, modifications, and novel applications of old ideas. The idea here isn't plagiarism, but inspiration, so don't get the wrong idea.

Newspaper Fail: Cut, Paste, Disaster.

One item in particular from his swipe file has kept us laughing for nearly five years. It is a full-color, full-page newspaper advertisement for a car dealership's inventory, which was obviously originally copied from a website. Why was this so obvious, you ask? Because underneath the images of each of the three "deeply-discounted" (wink, wink) cars that were featured in the advertisement was the following instruction:

Click HERE for more information.

That's right, you read that correctly: "Click HERE" in a newspaper advertisement. With a blue underlined hyperlink. Brilliant.

How's That for a 'Call to Action?'

Now, who ever heard of clicking a link in a newspaper advertisement? Click with what? Your finger? Your computer mouse? Your television remote control? Your garage door opener? What? Obviously, this was the result of careless copying and pasting of text or images from online ads to print advertisements.

What If Magazines Had Links, Too?

But, OH! What a great idea that would be! Imagine what would be possible if we could 'click' links in a magazine, book, newspaper, or letter, just like we do online, to take us to the next page, the next script, or the next featured content or video. What if we could?

Today, the truth is stranger than the fiction, or even stranger still than the marketing jokes and proofreading mistakes of a decade ago. Today, technology has caught up with us, and we are in fact able to 'click' printed links… by using QR Codes. And that's the most important thing to remember about using QR codes; no matter how deep, off-the-wall and complicated the ideas presented in this book become, this much is constant:

QR Codes enable us to firmly integrate our printed materials, including marketing items into our online materials, websites, videos, surveys, forms, emails, social media, and everything we do online, by allowing single click access to any online content from a printed "link."

And this is precisely the single and undeniable reason that QR codes are so popular, and so powerful. They make a printed piece of paper capable of supporting hyperlinks to web pages. Once there, the sky's the limit. Any content hosted online is up for grabs, fair game, available and viewable on a visitor's smart phone. So, when asked, *"Why do I need a QR Code?"* the answer is simple: To link your printed marketing media & assets to your online media assets. It's that simple. Write that down... there may be a quiz later.

Why Link My Print Ads & Website?

Now, this is an entirely different question. If you're running any type of organization, service, club, pseudo-business or real business, you're likely generating loads of paper documents, any or all of which can be prime real estate for a QR Code, to deliver just the right content, in the right context, and at the right moment. These can include:

- *Business Cards, Leaflets & Brochures*
- *Direct Mail Pieces, Post Cards, Letters*
- *Flyers, Inserts, etc.*
- *Faxes & Cover Sheets*
- *Fact Sheets, Proposals & White Papers*
- *Invoices & Contracts*
- *Business Letters (Marketing/Thanks)*
- *Magazine, Newspaper & other print media advertisements*
- *Packing Slips, Order Details, Address Labels*
- *Point-of-Sale Materials at your office*
- *Receipts, Packaging & Shipping Documents*
- *Information Sheets & Instruction Manuals*
- *Assorted signs & posters.*
- *Indoor and outdoor kiosks and advertising of all sorts.*

At the same time, your business likely spends a great deal of time, energy and money trying to drive traffic to your online content, whether for general brand recognition, or with specific goals of increasing 'Likes' or capturing visitor information for future marketing efforts. These include:

- *Your Home Page/ Landing Pages*
- *Your Social Media Pages (Facebook, Twitter, LinkedIn, YouTube)*
- *Product Demonstration Pages, including videos, manual & FAQs*
- *Menus, Product Descriptions & Listings*
- *eCommerce or Online Store Pages*
- *Contact forms for Email subscription lists, etc.*
- *Pure Response Tracking pages for cookie embedding & remarketing*
- *Affiliate program links*
- *In-app actions ("deep links")*

Link Them For Best Effect

So, a QR Code can be the vital bridge between what were, until recently, two completely different worlds: The printed domain and the online world, by enabling you to create clickable links from any of your printed marketing materials directly to your online media. Examples include:

- *For product purchasers: A QR Code on their packing slip can link directly to an instructional video on your YouTube Channel, and even tattle on the customer, recording whether they accessed the video or not, so that your technical support staff can know that they need to start over.*
- *For Contests & Promotions: A QR Code scan can link directly to an Online Entry Form, for single-scan mobile entries & registrations.*
- *For Direct Mail pieces: A unique QR Code identifies each individual mail recipient, so their scans can be attributable by name; get instant feedback on when the mail has arrived, which areas should be responding soon… which mail has mysteriously disappeared into the ether.*[1]
- *For Print Advertising: Supplement expensive Magazine or Newspaper advertisements with clickable links to even stronger offers, and easily monitor clicks and page visits.*
- *Even better: leverage remarketing to capture those visitors, and maintain top-of-mind consciousness.*
- *For Postings in Public Places: Scan for Wi-Fi login credentials, scan for the most updated schedules, specials & widget pricing.*
- *For Business Cards: Link to Social Media Profiles, Biography Page, etc, including media types that would be unavailable through any other means, such as videos, sound bites, animations, etc.*
- *For shipping and fulfillment services, a quick scan can record the shipping date for your widget.*

Just the Tip of the Iceberg

These, of course, are just the tip of the iceberg; a mere sampling of some of the ways that adding QR Codes to your printed business materials can enhance your business by linking it to supplemental information on the web. It's very difficult to imagine any business that can't take advantage of at least some of these benefits or incorporate some of these features into its marketing programs or operations. Thus, it's not surprising that businesses of all types have embraced QR Codes for their marketing materials, everything ranging from:

- *Billboards & Roadside Signs*
- *Web Pages & Online Video Trailers*
- *Avatars, Profile Photos & Featured Images*
- *Bumper Stickers & Vehicle Signage*
- *Sandwich Boards & Roadside Ads*
- *Direct Mail Response Tracking*

- *Checkout Counter and POS Materials*
- *Bus Stops & Community Notices*
- *vCards & MeCards that update contacts*
- *Wi-Fi & Network Logins*
- *Automatically adding calendar events*
- *And, of course all of the various other methods already mentioned above*

You Get the Picture

And this is just a quick sampling of what's possible with a QR Code. But, now that we've established the huge potential capabilities of QR Codes and begin to explore how to implement them, there are a few things that bear mentioning. First and foremost, an important question that will be dealt with fully in the next chapter:

When *not* to use a QR Code.

---

[1] *See the Advanced Techniques chapter for more information on how to go about accomplishing this.*

10. Don't Use QR Code...

Generally a QR Code can't work on a billboard, unless there is nothing there except for a QR Code. This advertisement also leverages the QR Code's ability to hide explicit content.

It is obvious, in writing a book such as this one, the utility of a QR Code and its absolute necessity for Mobile Marketing today is the ultimate message. But, make no mistake: there are many, *many* situations when use of a QR Code is misadvised, or even silly. In fact, much of the literature decrying the *"death of the QR Code"* and the like, both online and in print, is supported to a great degree by the lack of common sense and thought of many QR Code users employ (or fail to employ). when they utilize QR Codes without the slightest thought as to QR Code marketing *Best Practices.*

The Wrong Tool for the Job

Assorted Vehicle-Mounted QR Codes

A hammer is a really useful tool, unless you happen to be trying to unscrew a light bulb, or unless you hit yourself in the thumb. Just as you wouldn't use a hammer in the place of a screwdriver, or vice-versa, similarly, a QR Code shouldn't, and even cannot be used in many of the situations in which we see them used everyday. It's simply the wrong tool for the job. The following list is a brief synopsis of some places where it's not generally useful to use a QR Code. Of course, there are exceptions to every rule, but by and large, in nearly every case, these rules will hold true. Please internalize them and give them careful consideration before adding a QR Code in the following locations (coincidently, many of the top QR Code locations are on this list):

A QR Code on a Vehicle:

This is one of the most obvious places where a QR Code scan is not usually even possible, let alone safe, for assorted reasons:

- *The intended audience will not be close enough to scan it properly.*
- *The QR Code will need to be unreasonably large for scanning.*
- *The vehicle will most likely be in motion & scanning likely impossible.*
- *Timing. Will the person scanning have time to browse? (Honk! Honk!)*
- *Safety! If the message is intended for other drivers, it's misguided.*
- *Scanning's illegal. More areas enforce texting while driving bans every day.*
- *It's rarely implemented well, anyway. Call to Action? Explanation?*

It's a waste of space on the vehicle, because it just isn't possible to make the scan, in 95% of situations. A catchy name, slogan, vanity toll-free number, or easy-to-remember web address is preferable in nearly every conceivable case on vehicles.

When Will the QR Code Be Scanned?

In taking the time to think through an on-vehicle QR Code application, understand that although it is "quick and easy" to scan and use, long-distance, out-door applications are generally beyond their abilities. A QR Code takes some effort and time to scan. It isn't instantly and naturally recognized by our brains, as are other messages that we read everyday in traffic, like URLs, phone numbers, and advertisements on commercial vehicles.

The phone has to be grabbed, the app started, and of course the scan has to be made, usually unsuccessfully if it's being attempted in traffic. Further, in every application I see, there is no Call to Action (C2A), nor any reason given for a consumer to scan the QR Code, or even realize that what they were seeing was a QR Code intended for them to do something with, rather than a barcode for drive-through toll payment, or some other purpose. There's no reason to scan it unless you're a Mobile Marketing consultant and are curious. Take the examples from the figure in this chapter. Would you scan these, except for inclusion in a gallery of poorly executed QR Codes?

A QR Code on a Billboard?

For most of the same reasons as the above, and more QR Codes on billboards are simply misplaced.

- *The intended audience will never be close enough to scan it properly, unless the entire billboard is the QR Code, and they have someplace very safe to stand and attempt it.*[1]
- *While the Calvin Klein advertisement shown at the beginning of the chapter seems to be a better-than-average application of a massive QR Code on a billboard, there are several points to keep in mind:*
- *This is a VERY large billboard, and very low to the ground (the bottom edge is approximately 10 feet from the ground). Most billboards are far higher from the ground & far narrower vertically, making a QR Code scan next to impossible.*
- *It's far closer to its intended audience as a typical billboard, and meant to be scanned by nearby pedestrians… and not distant vehicle drivers.*
- *The QR Code must take up the entire billboard. There really isn't room for any advertising message at all… just a tease; which is a stunt that can only work when the QR Code is in its infancy. If every advertisement could only be viewed by scanning a QR Code, we would all breathe a sigh of relief at being liberated from ads.*

In this case, the QR Code also masks questionable content, containing flashes of nudity, which certainly could not be shown on the billboard, either via video or photographic images. In short, it's inappropriate[2]. This is both a positive and a negative, in that it provides both a great example of using the QR Code to bridge to print media, specifically by linking to online content that may not necessarily be permitted in the QR Code's location, but it is also a cautionary example of an application that flirts with controversy and risks public censure… a long-standing advertising hook, but a bad move for most brands, regardless of the fact that "sex sells."

Although this is held up as a case of a single well done billboard QR Code (in pure theory), well done is certainly not the rule. Rather, botched attempts are the norm, such as the below QR Code, which was found at the side of a congested strip of I-75 outside of Tampa, Florida, on a very small billboard, hidden behind a tree, flashing into view momentarily for traffic moving at 70 miles per hour… a quadruple no-no.

QR Codes on Roadside Signs.

Who precisely is the target audience for this roadside advertisement? Drivers?

Figure 2: Who can possibly scan?

A photo was only possible by using a camera phone at maximum zoom, and making multiple attempts all week long (my co-pilot took the shot, I swear). Still, I have yet to successfully scan it, even off-line by trying to upload the picture. Not only is the QR Code impossible to scan, but the advertisement is generally quite bad. What kind of company is this? And what service is being offered? When on earth would I call them? What would they do for me?

One of my favorite misapplications is on a sign carried by a "kinetic outdoor" roadside advertiser holding a sign. He would constantly toss and shake the sign to attract attention – in fact, that's the whole point of the job. In any case, he's in constant motion, and I'll bet he's never succeeded in getting a scan. The target audience of such advertising is obviously vehicle drivers. So, all of the above criticisms apply once again. Not only is it futile and impossible to scan, but also it is unsafe.

A double-whammy: a QR Code on a fairly small billboard, hidden behind a tree, positioned to be only visible for drivers on an interstate highway. Or hitchhikers.

Figure 3 Speed Limit 70mph

Safety! If the message is intended for other drivers, it's misguided, unless it links to a traffic-accident checklist, which might be useful when you make them crash.

Regarding Online QR Codes:

While there is no absolutely pressing reason not to use a QR Code online, there are certainly very, *very* few conceivable reasons in favor of using one. Think about this for a moment: The purpose of a QR Code is to make printed links "clickable" so that they can link to online media: that's the primary purpose of using one. If your target audience is already online at your web page, why ask them to pull out their phone and scan? This is silly for a number of reasons:

- *If they're on the site, a simple web link is just as effective; usually more effective. Provide a clickable link that they can use to access the content you'd like them to see.*
- *If you'd like to use an attractive image or call-to-action, you can do a lot better than a QR Code; since you're online, anything can be clickable, so the sky's the limit. Use a photo or a nice inviting button. Why use a QR Code?*
- *If they're on your website already, there's no reason not to simply have the desired content on the current page; why try to divert them to another location?*
- *Your visitor may already be browsing from a mobile device, and have no other mobile device to use to scan.*

- *Your user is certainly already browsing from his or her preferred device. Why ask them to change devices?*

That last one is the silliest idea of all: picture your site visitor borrowing a friend's phone to scan your QR Code from the screen of his own, to continue the visit on his friend's phone. What?

QR Codes must generally be much larger on screen than in print, in order to scan properly. Why take up space online with an ugly QR Code (and most people still insist on keeping them as ugly as possible), when its job is already done: getting the mobile user to your website Landing Page. Further, why not employ an eye-catching graphic or image that the user can simply click, and keep using the site as they chose to, rather than potentially asking them to switch devices. If they're using a desktop, that's the better browsing experience already! Don't send them to an inferior mobile version. If they're mobile, they can't scan it anyway, unless they borrow a friend's phone. It's comical, but I've seen QR Codes frequently included on Landing Pages that can only be accessed via QR Code scans. Ponder that one.

Further, depending on a number of factors, including the app they use, their computer screen type & refresh rate, the QR Code may be difficult to scan. A number of apps I use, notably NeoReader for iPhone has some difficulty scanning from the computer screen. If a visitor is already on your site, using the device of their choice, just use simple web links (HTML hyperlinks) or clickable image links to guide them to the intended content. Don't attempt to make them switch devices, or try to scan one QR Code off the screen of one device with a second device, or any other such absurd acrobatics. I suppose that one could envision an entire chain of mobile visitors, each using an on-screen QR Code to pass a site on to the next, ad infinitum. Not likely.

All of the same difficulties apply to a QR Code used on television, and to a lesser extent, one on a movie screen.[3] LED & LCD screens are generally better than CRTs[4], but you'll limited control over the screen on which your audience views your QR Code. Use due diligence.

Noteworthy Exceptions for Online Use

As with any rule, there is certainly room for exceptions, just not many. A QR Code can be a great idea for any web page that is highly likely to be actually printed for later study, reading, reference or duplication off-line. So, this could apply to many Blog items (and is the reason that some Blogs include a QR Code on every page, dynamically generated to link back to the page). Online recipes or instructions posted to sites similar to Pinterest.com, Ask.com, sites with maps and directions that are intended to be printed, such as Google Maps, or Do-It-Yourself sites that give users instructions for tasks that they can print out & follow, etc. Once a user has printed them, anyone with a copy of the instructions can easily return to the content with just a quick snap, and access it on their own... with a QR Code on downloadable or printable materials, especially useful and durable goods, your website just went viral, with an army of promoters circulating it everywhere, free of charge.

Examples could include downloadable worksheets, checklists, paper forms, etc, all of which would do well to have a QR Code printed on them, to brand them, ensuring that anyone who uses future photocopies of the original printouts will be able to return to the website with a quick snap.

The same applies for online fact sheets, cheat sheets, "working aids," teacher's handouts, various forms for enrollment. Adobe Acrobat Professional has excellent QR Code generation abilities, to provide precisely this functionality, and even more: Generate a QR Code based on content of a form field, for example.

If there is little likelihood that the page will be printed, there is probably no reason to include a QR Code. Common sense dictates that if a visitor is browsing your site on a desktop system, there is no reason to switch. If they are comfortable with their mobile device and are already browsing your site via a mobile device, as I do for all my Facebooking, how would they scan it anyway? I fail to see the logic. Are you listening, BofA?

---

[1] *See endnote 1, above. A billboard 300 feet away/high should have a QR Code 45 feet wide/tall for proper scanning. Smaller than that, and it may not be possible to scan it at all.*
[2] *Which is why, you may have noticed, that I corrupted the QR Code so that it wouldn't scan. The content at the other end was simply not something that I felt obligated to share.*
[3] *In Chapter 9, we discuss QR Codes on TV; suboptimal, but with care, anything is possible. Campaigns mentioned there had extensive marketing run-up and testing, as part of a large, professionally-run campaign.*
[4] *Light-Emitting Diode, Liquid-Crystal Display, and Cathode-Ray Tube computer monitors, respectively. Depending on context, any of these can make a QR Code scan very difficult.*

11. QR Codes Gone Bad

"Mobile Tagging is here to stay,
only the bad implementations will die."
- Tappinn.com

The above is the single best characterization I've encountered, expressing precisely what's wrong with marketing using QR Codes. Dim-witted implementations are the standard. Why is the QR Code done so very wrong, most of the time? Why can't anyone bother to tell the uninitiated what this code means and what to do with it? Would that be so difficult?

My speculation is that because the QR Code is new, hip, and high-tech, it's having a bandwagon effect. Everybody needs one. In the 1970s, you needed a business card, in the 1980s a 1-800 number, in the 1990s a website, in the 2000s an IPO, and now you've got to have a QR Code or you're just not hip, 'with-it', or technically competent.

Unfortunately, there are larger problems than simply misadvised and awkward QR Code applications; after all, who am I to judge where a QR Code should and should not be. There are probably another ten self-styled marketing experts just like me, lined up around the corner to tell you that the truth is the precise opposite of what I'm writing. To each his own, right? This is a new, ill-defined and confusing technology, so how can we expect that everything done is going to be perfect, from day one?

Well, I'm not referring here to merely *misadvised* or *distasteful* material that could be done better; *that* was the previous chapter. In this chapter, we're discussing QR Code applications that simply don't work at all… an epidemic of incompetence of such disastrous proportions that it has actually given the QR Code itself a bad rap.

How bad does the driving have to be, if people can't help but blame the cars? Anyone reluctant to adopt the new code scan technologies has my sympathies, since the marketers pushing QR Codes aren't making it very enjoyable or easy for them. What's the problem? Failed applications are so widespread that sometimes it is occasionally difficult to find QR Codes that look and work right. And I should know, because I've never seen one that I didn't scan... make that *attempt to scan.*

QR Code Failure Compilation:

I've assembled in the following pages a photo montage of a dozen or so QR codes that I've photographed and scanned, having found them all over the place. I've scanned them in traffic (while safely stopped dead in gridlock, I should add), I've scanned them on billboards, I've scanned them in parking lots, on restaurant signs, on cars, on park benches, on bus stops, and on signs posted all over. And, as someone knowledgeable in using QR codes for response tracking purposes, I'm baffled as to why they don't work. This applies equally to Fortune 500 companies and mom and pop sandwich shops. **One important caveat for this section: You'll have to take my word for it that some of them *worked.* Most marketing campaigns are short-term, and most media are weekly periodicals or mail pieces, so are disposable: with a service life of days to weeks. It's certainly not fair to expect them to be kept online for years, just for demonstration purposes, although it would be nice. So, keep in mind in attempting to scan these that there's no reason for them to work still.**

The Link to Nowhere.

Scan Failure at Staples. No one's immune. Still doesn't work.

Congratulations, you've educated yourself on QR Codes, chosen a cool service with all the bells and whistles, and created some QR Codes and stuck them on what you need! Now, it's just a waiting game until the eager scanning public gets curious and starts hitting your Landing Page. But they don't. Maybe you get a call from the marketing department, or the head of advertising, or your spouse, saying that they received today's newspaper and tried to scan the cute little codey-thing that you excitedly mentioned working on for the past month and it went nowhere.

Of course the first and worst mistake to make when employing QR Codes is for them to simply not work. I know, this is obvious, but unfortunately needs bearing out. There are dozens of things that can go wrong and render a QR Code unreadable, and nearly all of these things are completely and totally avoidable (most having nothing at all to do with the QR Code itself); There's simply no reason for them to happen to you. The following are examples of these.

Wrong or non-existent URLs

Mistakes happen. That's why testing should be a part of the process at every step along the way. Every new QR Code should have been scanned by multiple devices, including at least one each of the big four: Windows, Blackberry, Android & iPhone operating systems. Not only should this never have happened, but, the following steps will also ensure that this blunder is easily and instantly correctible.

The following are two prime examples of blunders by major corporations; Fortune 500 companies with all the resources in the world, making inexplicable blunders. QR Codes on merchandise promise reviews and consumer information… but don't resolve.

At one of the Big Three office supply stores, every printer, scanner, and office machine has a QR Code that promises "customer reviews and more information." The first several I tried were non-functional, so I gave up. Two-thirds simply did not work.

A newspaper advertisement promises a Sneak Peak of a new movie, but all content is inactive and marked "Coming Soon…"

A QR Code scan promises access to a mobile site, which is non-existent (though fixed within a few days).

Promised Content is Missing

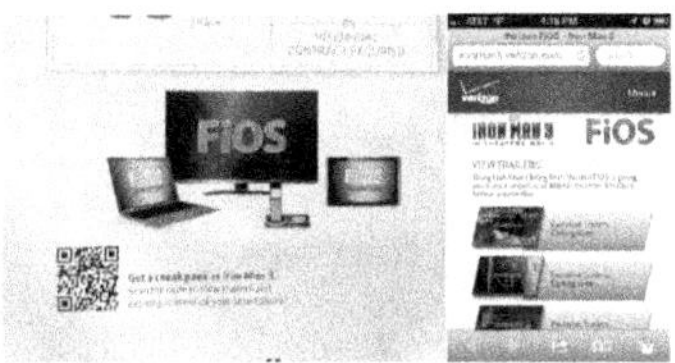

Big Budget campaign that doesn't deliver what it promises.

In this advertisement incorporating a QR Code, the online content is an excellent, very professional mobile website intended to host (most importantly) the promised content of a "sneak peek at Iron Man 3." Unfortunately, the content simply isn't present; all the links for trailers read, "Coming Soon" and no video clips are available, nor was it later made available for the entire 1-week shelf life of this advertisement, printed in a weekly coupon mailer. [1]This illustrates just how easy it can be to undermine an entire campaign by poorly troubleshooting the mobile site before printing. In preserving this error for this book project, I saved the QR Code far longer than the shelf life of this mailer; thus, I may in fact have been the only person alive to actually watch these trailers as intended, by visiting the Landing Page.

The day this campaign hit, there was no site present. (it was corrected, after customers complained).

If this can be done in an advertisement printed by the largest Direct Mail company in the United States (Valassis), in a coordinated campaign between a major Hollywood movie studio, a Fortune 100 phone company, and an entertainment giant like Marvel, it can happen to anyone. But, it need not. Landing Pages simply *must* be prepared for visitors and tested to ensure that they are functional. Do not print until everything is ready. It's that simple.

Control Your Landing Page.

Never direct a QR Code to any URL that you don't control. Otherwise, you risk having the rug pulled out from under you with no notice. This also means don't direct the traffic to your home page, as it will rarely be optimized for the current campaign, unless this current campaign is all you've got, and all you're ever going to have. This is the whole concept of a Landing Page – a dedicated entry point for a visitor who 'lands' on your website, with a specific, dedicated message dictated by the reason for their visit, what was promised them, and which campaign they are responding to.

I see repeatedly applications where a company has directed QR Code scanners to its home page directly. In fact, the very last QR Code I scanned today before typing this line was one of these. There are many issues with this, all of which can be resolved, save two. First and foremost, unless your company has one service, one offer, and one message, and never intends to improve or grow, then the home page is not the right Landing Page. It is unlikely that your home page is the place for a focused offer for the QR Code-scanning consumer.

Second, and this can be overcome, although most don't: when all traffic is directed to your home page, how are you quantifying the success of the Mobile Marketing campaign? Who is responding via QR Code and who just woke up and decided to visit the site today, or found you through a search engine? Or used a bookmark? Or responded to another, completely unrelated advertisement or campaign? Take these two QR Codes, both of which I received in the mail, on mini-flyers bundled together with other coupons from mailing giant Val-Pak Direct Marketing Systems (ie, Val-Pak), which sends their signature blue envelopes stuffed with offers to nearly every home in America on the 2nd to last Wednesday of the month:

The publisher of the first QR Code made both of these mistakes, and has no way of determining what traffic is directly attributable to their QR Code-response campaign, because the response is not individually trackable. They are right now wondering whether it was worth putting the QR Code on there, and even if they discern a small spike in their traffic, they'll truly never know; Not only whether the QR Code was effective, but whether the entire ad placement was worthwhile. The addition of a simple URL Query String could have identified the traffic as well.

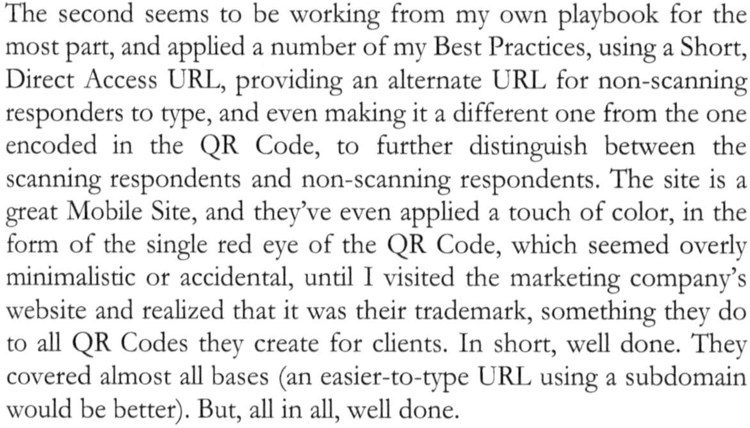
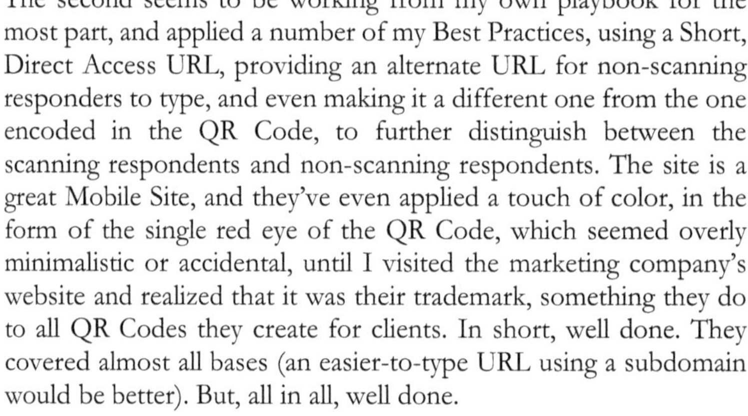

Scan this QR Code with your smart phone or type in http://tappin.com/p/31748

The second seems to be working from my own playbook for the most part, and applied a number of my Best Practices, using a Short, Direct Access URL, providing an alternate URL for non-scanning responders to type, and even making it a different one from the one encoded in the QR Code, to further distinguish between the scanning respondents and non-scanning respondents. The site is a great Mobile Site, and they've even applied a touch of color, in the form of the single red eye of the QR Code, which seemed overly minimalistic or accidental, until I visited the marketing company's website and realized that it was their trademark, something they do to all QR Codes they create for clients. In short, well done. They covered almost all bases (an easier-to-type URL using a subdomain would be better). But, all in all, well done.

Don't Over-Do It.

One doesn't have to browse long to find plenty of examples. This is one of the worst mistakes to make, particularly for a small business owner or serious salesperson. It's also an exceptionally common one, even by Fortune 500 companies… to include those who make the QR Code-capable smart phones: Overcomplicating it. Just because you can, doesn't mean you should. Technical prowess is no match for good common sense.

I was recently browsing through the November 2012 issues of Entertainment Weekly and Motor Trend Magazine, among several others. In the Entertainment Weekly, I was surprised to discover that there were three QR Codes in separate (though nearly-identical) ads for an HTC phone. The advertisement was interesting, offering to automatically detect my Smart Phone manufacturer & model and generate a trade-in offer toward a new HTC Smart Phone. However, the server was too busy to actually deliver, and it took several frustrating scans to get it to work; it was only rescued from an appearance in my failure gallery because of my astonishing persistence; I *really* wanted to see what it did! Also, all three advertisements landed on the same page, certainly a missed opportunity to test response to differing ads.[2]

The Truly Defective

Of course, the second most classic blunder in QR codes is the unscannable bar code. By 'unscannable', I don't mean difficult to scan because of data density, size, or other factors, since these are at least potentially scannable. What I'm talking about is the truly unscannable: QR codes that point to non-existent web addresses, or that generate error pages, because the original URLs were not encoded properly. The office-supply store debacle mentioned earlier in the chapter is a prime example of that.

Figure 4 A good implementation.

Now, I address more of the specific reasons for this in later chapters, but there's always the unscannable QR Code: reasons include poor planning: this one was printed on what would be a fold. This shouldn't be enough to damage the QR Code beyond recognition, but poor print quality (inkjet is far inferior to laser, definitely a factor here) makes the QR Code nearly impossible to scan. But I'm a bit more persistent than the average consumer, and did get it to scan, only to find that it was coded with the wrong information: After trying every possible thing I could, I was finally able to get a good scan from this code. What was the URL? Not a URL at all. Just a number: "1128287787878". Perhaps a scan error? Perhaps a coding error? In any case, a universal failure from the QR Code angle. Personally, I was expecting a website.

For the record, this mailer was produced and sent to my wife by a *very* well-known direct mail marketing company, for a Tampa, Florida-area Toyota dealership.

Always Plan for Errors

Plan to fail... *gracefully*. That sounds defeatist. I'm not a pessimist, but a realist. Nobody hopes to crash-land a flaming 747 jumbo jet at 500 mph in the ocean. Nonetheless, airplane factories mass-produce and install fire extinguishers, oxygen masks, seat-cushion floatation devices, life-rafts, inflatable escape slides, survival kits, emergency beacons in as many airplanes as they install landing gears and exit stairs, and for good reason. Sometimes stuff happens, no matter how hard we try to get things right. When it does, all your great planning becomes irrelevant. Fortune favors the prepared.

For the same reason, I always recommend that all QR codes (and, all URLs, in fact, especially short codes) be created with the potential to be re-coded on the back end, to point to a different site, as needed, even after mailing or other deployment/installation, using an appropriate means within ones technical abilities.

This can rescue an entire mail campaign, web campaign, or any marketing campaign that relies heavily on QR Codes for response or response tracking. This way, even in the worst-case-scenario of a blunder that deletes or changes a Landing Page, the QR code can always be re-named, re-purposed, and directed to the correct location, or a backup location. There are several ways of doing this, each with its respective benefits and drawbacks.

- *A subdomain Landing Page is ideal, and meets all Best Practice requirements, but in the event of problems, can take from several hours to several days to redirect using your web hosting controls. The benefit to this is that it is a single stop, with no latency (delays and redirects). More on latency later.*
- *Another option would be a Javascript, PHP, or ASP.NET page redirect. This certainly adds a small amount of delay and latency, but can be reconfigured in seconds.*
- *A URL Shortener is another method for doing this, as will be explained in the later chapter on URL Shortening. This is less optimum than using a subdomain[3], but has one great benefit for rainy days: it can be swapped to a new location in seconds. Also, the technical demands for this are the most minimal. Any layman can do it.*

This, of course, is not only applicable in situations of errors, but also to changes in offers or text. Unlike hard-copy mail or print ads, which once sent, are out there and must be honored through expiration, at the risk of alienating customers or causing legal problems, an advertisement viewed through a QR Code (or short URL) that can be edited, can be re-directed daily, weekly, or even hourly, to a new offer, with just a few keystrokes, and even by a novice. Compare this with the expense and technical know-how needed to replace or recode a specific webpage indicated by the coded URL with new content if it proves problematic, or re-create a new Landing Page in the correct location, while coping with ruining any other links pointing to this same location. A nightmare. It may not even be possible to re-code the Landing Page, for example if something of value is located there, such as one's home page, that can't simply be deleted or replaced to make room for your landing page.

This can even fix acts of God: delayed mail, rained-out events, etc, are situations where you may want to change your landing page in a hurry.

There are several solid strategies for accomplishing this, as outlined above. Solutions range from very easy, to not terribly difficult.

The simplest is a redirectable URL shortener. QRstuff.com allows redirects for archived QR Codes that use its qrs.ly shortener. As does the YOURLS system described in later chapters. Most for-fee subscription services allow changes to the shortened codes.

First Choice: The DNS Solution:

The ideal way to do this is the setup your web server's DNS (Domain Name Service) to reflect the desired location. Without delving into a lengthy explanation of internet protocol, when a web page is requested, a directory is consulted to ascertain where the requested page is physically located, in order to retrieve it. This is part of the process for every page requested from the internet, so it is the only solution that doesn't add an extra step, potential latency, or a potential point of failure to the process. While any other solutions catch and redirect the visitor's browser, this is the only solution that doesn't redirect the browser... it simply directs it properly the first time. Editing your DNS records isn't very difficult, but can be done wrong, creating problems for your website. It can also vary depending on the current configuration and what else is being done with the site.

For the non-tech-savvy who won't be making manual changes to their DNS zone files, if your hosting allows you access through Cpanel, Plesk, or another hosting manager, allows a very smooth creation of subdomains and one-step redirect that updates your DNS settings automatically.

The sole *potential* drawback to using the web server's DNS settings to direct the browser is that the web server may have a TTL (Time-to-Live) of anywhere from 10 minutes to 48 hours. Usually these changes happen within an hour. But, frankly, the top-level domain you use, country of registration, host company policies, can all have bearing on this. So, there is the potential for you to be locked out and have no way to make a fast change in a pinch, ie, should you discover a really disastrous error during a campaign (say, for example, the two hottest voting days during a contest you've sponsored, or the two days that a very expensive mailer you've sent is in homes). In a bind, that will be the longest 48 hours of your life. But, to be fair, it is usually done within 10 minutes.

But, barring the need for a desperate on-the-fly change (caused by errors elsewhere), this TTL issue isn't cause for concern. If you're simply looking to re-use a QR Code in which there was some investment of time or money (professional re-touching or validation, etc), this is the ideal way to redirect it. Simply encode a dedicated subdomain of your domain name into the QR Code matrix, and then redirect the code's landing page using the DNS settings, for the service life of the QR Code. Very economical and efficient, the "right way" to do this.

Javascript Solution:

Finally, this can be done easily with just one line of Javascript as well. Note that, unlike the previous two examples, this code should be inserted into a page of well-formed HTML: ideally between the <head></head> tags, or between the <body></body> tags is you must, so for clarity, the entire page is shown.


```
<html>
   <head>
      <script>
         window.location.assign("http://www.new.com/page.
html");
      </script>
   </head>
   <body>
         <!- main body of the page goes here, but will not -
>
         <!- be displayed; the page will jump to this URL->
   </body>
</html>
```

The PHP Solution:

The below is a complete PHP file that will redirect to a location of your choosing, any web traffic requesting the page, in but a single line of code. Save the following (and no other text or whitespace of any type) into a text file, and upload it to your web server as the landing page coded into your QR Code:

```
<?php
         header('Location: http://www.new.com/page.html');
 ?>
```

Microsoft ASP.NET Solution:

Similarly, an Active Server Pages setup allows the same.[4]

```
<%
         Response.Redirect "http://www.new.com/page.html"
%>
```

URL Shortener Solution:

If any of these leave you bewildered, and the thought of writing any code, tinkering with your web server settings makes you cringe, then the simplest solution for you is to code a dynamic (ie, one that can be changed) URL into your QR Code. By using YOURLS, UnitagLive.com, or QRStuff.com's dynamic feature, you can change out the destination of a shortened URL instantly. It's the non-techie's solution to getting this job done the easy way.

And, though I don't recommend it as the ideal, its not that bad at all. You'll get metrics on click throughs and browser info, as well as a great UI to monitor things.

---

[1] *At press time, several weeks after the mailer hit homes, the promised trailers were available. Undoubtedly, I was the only person alive who was still interested and waiting.*

[2] *I assume that a company as tech-savvy as HTC would have been using Google Analytics or a similar analytics method to measure the sources of web traffic to the landing page. Three near-identical advertisements directing to the same landing page is a terrible waste. They could easily have measured response to the three ads individually, by appending a "Query String" to the URL encoded in the QR Code. For example: http://mysite.com/?source=ad1 (Entertainment Weekly Ad #1) versus http://mysite.com/?source=ew_ad2 (Entertainment Weekly Ad #2). The information after the question mark would be ignored by the user's browser, and the web page displayed to the user. However, Google Analytics would note and record the traffic source. In fact, you could even use GA's tags for this, such as "utm_campaign=", and specify the campaign name in your GA dashboard, to know instantly which of the three ads performed best. In marketing circles, this is called A/B Testing.*

[3] *The jury is still out with me as to the best way to do this. It's always a judgment call. A subdomain will always be the best for many reasons detailed in the next chapter: just make sure that you do things right, and won't need emergency corrections; They may take too long. Easy, right? Wrong. I've been around long enough to know that things go wrong, and using an instantly re-directable short URL keeps my blood pressure low and my sleep secure.*

[4] *While the author is highly experienced in PHP development, quoting ASP code is more academic.*

12. QR Codes Done Right

Now that we've had a chance to touch on what constitutes bad QR Code marketing practices, and identified some colossal failures to avoid as cautionary examples, we come to a discussion of Best Practices in QR Code marketing. It is these best practices that have been sorely lacking from literature on QR Codes, as well as the implementations resulting from this lack. Fully harnessing the value of a QR Code as a popular bridge linking printed media (or even televised media) to one's online assets and resources requires a number of careful steps to encourage the successful scanning of the QR Codes, best functionality of the QR Codes, as well as the best-crafted user experience after the scan, and the best follow-up response after their response.

Make Sure Your QR Codes Work

Generally, QR Codes will be coded properly, when generated by online systems. But, simply because you generated a QR Code online and downloaded it, don't put full and total faith in the generator. The application is only as good as the programmer who created it, and the operator who used it. There's really no way to know how closely the programmer adhered to the ISO 18004 specification, or how error-free the coding is, whether the proper URL or other information was provided, etc. Testing is always vital.

One way to always be sure to get the highest-quality encoding is to use DENSO WAVE INCORPORATED's own QR Code generator, which is available for free download with registration at www.denso-wave.com. Starting with the best encoding is a great start to ensuring that your QR Codes will work under all conditions. Beyond that, the rules and concepts of ensuring that your QR Codes function properly are addressed in later chapters, since they are really most important as you begin adding high levels of customization, or artistically compromising your QR Codes to make Designer QR Codes. The basics of how to do it are covered in the next chapter.

Mobile Websites Are Essential:

Of course, despite being the entire topic of this book, it must be remembered that the QR Code is ultimately only the gateway to the online media. There are at least 26 vitally important points, the neglect of which will result in suboptimal results at best for a campaign using QR Codes. These are detailed in the Chapter on *Best Practices.* But, by far, the most important, and most neglected, factor is the post-scan user experience that is accessed by scanning the QR Code.

It cannot be said enough: the web page accessed by scanning your QR Codes absolutely, positively, must be a mobile-optimized website. The mobile user simply has a different device, different usage habits, different hardware, different realities and capabilities than an online user with a desktop system. The entire concept of

© 2010 Warbasse Design

website and Landing Page design pre-dates Mobile Marketing, and the reduction in screen and keyboard size, bandwidth, processing power that mobile devices necessitate cannot be ignored.

I had a great opportunity recently to interview Philip Warbasse, CEO of Warbasse Media, whose company has run mobile marketing campaigns for giants such as Citibank and HBO. His company is responsible for the "First QR Code to appear on Television," the gruesome QR Code pictured here, which links to a trailer for HBO Televisions hit series True Blood and was run during ABC's Lost (more interesting in the color version of this book). His company, 2dprint.com also just finished work on a QR Code campaign for another upcoming major Hollywood film (which can't be mentioned until a year after the release date), and has built a name in Hollywood for marketing campaigns for motion pictures.

Philip's firm has honed Mobile Marketing to a world class level; they view the QR Code correctly as simply the vehicle by which a customer arrives on your site: The thrust of their business is hosting the Landing Pages to which the QR Code-scanning visitor is directed, and crafting the User Experience on the sites. Of course, this necessarily means a mobile-optimized website. Moreover, he echoes many of my own basic criteria, adding one more that I've had to include: *Direct linking to content without redirection.*

- *Mobilized: The absolute necessity of mobile-optimized content.*
- *Direct URL Access: Rather than through URL shortener/redirect*
- *Deeply Trackable: The value of trackability and attribution of the user's entire visit, rather than merely a click-through count.*

The first two of these factors are discussed at length herein. But Philip also enlightened me to several other vital factors in reaping the biggest returns from mobile marketing. Because this book is intended for laymen and do-it-yourself-ers, much of the advice in this book has focuses on the most basic metrics available from URL shorteners (such as date & time of click, location of clicker, mobile device Operating System, etc).

Rightly, Phillip isn't fond of them as the sole means of quantifying response from mobile marketing campaigns. A potent reason for his preference for a direct-access solution is *Latency*. The more intermediate stops that a visitor takes on their way to your site, the more time it takes for them to arrive at each stop, and be re-directed to the next location. Causes of latency delays can include:

- *Complicated graphics or animations (load time)*
- *Content Management System processing time*
- *Excessive web traffic (or alternately, insufficient bandwidth)*
- *On-Page Scripting (scripts that request/wait to receive info)*
- *Excessive Redirects*
- *Server errors*
- *Many, many more potential factors.*

Not only do the above actions take time (thus placing you at the mercy of your visitor's patience and attention span), but it also adds complexity to the process, creating new "fail points" where a malfunction or high web traffic could bring the system to a halt. Obviously, more bandwidth is better, and keeping graphics, scripts, CMS widgets, etc, to a minimum is best. But, adding redirects, such as an alternate URL that forwards, or deliberately adding a step using a URL Shortener are two easy ones that can should be eliminated when technically feasible. Additionally, when used only for click-through metrics, a URL Shortener is rarely the right solution; rather, it is simply the easiest solution.

So, measuring response solely by using a URL shortener may be easy to set up for the typical small-business user; but, there are several definite drawbacks of these types of systems, in that they only record the moment that the webpage was accessed, as the visitor is forwarded on to the Landing Page. What happens next remains a mystery. Philip's analogy is that of being the ticket-taker at a movie theater; you get to see everyone on the way in, but have no idea what they're doing inside, how long they stay, which movie they're watching, how they enjoyed it, whether they purchased popcorn and drinks, who they're telling about it, etc.

The Multi-Dimensional Solution

His company's managed solutions shift the paradigm away from this "click & forward" counting method to fully-hosted Landing Page solutions that send a user directly to a Landing Page, rather than indirectly through a URL Shortener, and provide deep, multi-dimensional analytics, through the visitor's entire session, and not simply the moment of arrival.

A full analytical solution, such as Google Analytics will give all of the same information, but far deeper, dimensional information, as well, including a click-by-click navigation map of every page a user visited. This way, more than simply a count of clicks and operating system demographics is available; rather, full records of a user's visit become possible:

- *All of the above information: Date & Time of visit, location information (potentially latitude & longitude), OS, etc, as well as…*
- *Each page on the site that the user visited.*
- *The length of time spent on each.*
- *"Focus," or items the user considered clicking by mouse hovering.*
- *Resulting Social Media shares, etc.*
- *ROI Calculations based on purchases made or subscriptions*

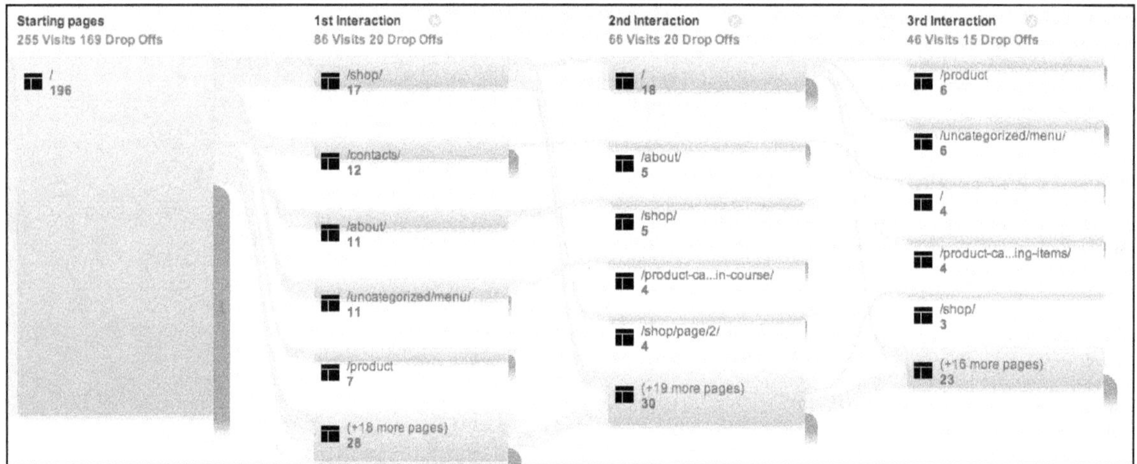

Figure 5 Google Analytics Visitor Flow

- *Virtually any information about a user's visit.*

For in-depth tracking of user visits and actions, Google Analytics remains the de facto standard in web tracking and analytics. And, as always, it is free of charge, one of the best-kept non-secrets on the web. Set up an account in a few minutes, and register your sites to receive a unique tracking code that you can add to all the pages of your website so that visitor activity is reported.

This information is then available in various formats in your Google Analytics dashboard. Adding the Google Analytics code, or as Philip recommends, the Google *Mobile* Analytics code is the way to get the best data on who is visiting your site, how long they stay, what they are doing, what they want to do, which pages they like and which pages send them scurrying.

For example, above is a sample diagram generated by the Google Analytics dashboard, tracing the flow of 196 site visitors as they progressively navigate through one of my websites. This is of immense value in determining which pages are "sticky" and encourage users to continue to read or browse and which pages cause visitors to simply leave. Taller blocks indicate more visitors and longer stays, red "drop-off" columns show the page where they lost interest and left the site. For example, this diagram shows clearly that visitors who selected my *About* or *Shop* pages all stayed on the site, whereas many visitors to other pages left on their next click.[1]

This Isn't Always Easy.

Like all of the other strategies outlined in this book, the general thrust of these techniques can be incorporated into the marketing plans of businesses of all sizes in many ways, with a bit of know-how and leg-work. But, it certainly isn't for everyone. A small bit of technical ability is involved, as direct editing of your website's HTML files is usually going to be necessary. Alternately, if a website is built using a robust CMS system (such as Joomla, Drupal, or my own go-to CMS, Wordpress), this can be accomplished even by a total novice using an easily-configurable analytics plugin. Just provide the plugin with your *property ID* from your Google Analytics dashboard, and your tracking code will be automatically inserted on all pages to track them. For advanced ROI calculations and integration of different campaigns, some learning and tweaking is necessary, but for the most basic functionality, including the above example, all that's necessary is a brief setup.

Options for a Mobile Website

The absolutely necessity of a Mobile Website has been addressed earlier. All traffic generated by a QR Code scan will be from a mobile device, and so you will be *Mobile Marketing*. As such, you will need a mobile-optimized website, or at a minimum a mobile mini-site or Landing Page. For crafting mobile sites, there are a number of options available for quickly creating mobile-optimized versions of websites with little cost and little technical knowledge.

So, there should be no reason why having a mobile-optimized site is out of reach for anyone. Some suggested options for low-cost and even free Mobile web solutions, that can be assembled very quickly, usually in one sitting, are:

- ***HowToGoMo.com*** *(By Google) Google's entry into the market, which is (as of press time) offering free mobile sites. Google's entry further provides many excellent fact sheets and white papers that give simple, in-depth advice, guidelines, and instructions for putting together the best possible mobile site for any organization.*
- ***Onbile.com****: An excellent and easy-to-use service with a robust free version. Excellent navigation and very organic look.*
- ***Dudamobile.com:*** *Another excellent submission, which is available free as an add-on application through several hosting services, and configurable directly within the hosting interface. Simply click "Activate Mobile Site," (or some such) from your hosting control panel (when logged into your account at the site), and you've got a mobile site instantly, with a WYSIWYG editor. It doesn't get better than automatic. DudaMobile.com has my own recommendation, for the sake of simplicity for the user. By simply turning on the Mobile Website application in my GoDaddy Hosting panel, I was able to instantly create a mobile version of my site, without having to edit it at all. GoDaddy automatically configured a re-direct to the mobile site for any visitors using mobile devices.*[2]
- ***Mofuse.com:*** *Mozilla's entry into this field, and another extremely easy-to-use mobile website generator. Although, as demonstrated in the previous chapter, technical hiccups aren't necessarily handled gracefully.*[3]
- *Generally speaking, most hosting companies, including GoDaddy, HostGator, BlueHost, and many more, offer one or more of the above services as one-click add-ons to hosting service (usually at no charge) to generate and redirect a mobile version of your site to any visitors, based on device*

detection, so you may, in all likelihood be set up already to take advantage… you just didn't know it.

Alternatives to a Mobile Website

With most of the above sites, you'll be able customize a site to suit your business, most likely based on your current site, but modified to meet the needs of a visitor using a smaller screen. At worst, you will be provided with a code snippet, a few lines of Hypertext Markup Language (HTML) code to add by hand into your web page's HTML code. What this will do is detect mobile devices attempting to visit, and invisibly re-direct all mobile devices that try to access your site to the mobile version of the site, which is of exceptional value; all mobile users should be automatically redirected to a mobile site, since it's a rare mobile device with the resolution and screen size to adequately display the average webpage.

But, even if you don't have the ability to do this and the thought of hand-editing your web pages fills you with terror, you can always use the Direct URL of the mobile site as the destination Landing Page for your QR Code, utilizing the site *separately*. They are, in most cases, separate sites anyway, after all, and the illusion of them being one site is really just due to the behind-the-scenes redirection magic. So, if this is asking too much of your technically abilities, keep in mind that it isn't entirely necessary. Just send the QR Code scanners to the mobile version, preferably by coding a subdomain like "http://m.yoursite.com/your_offer" for your mobile site ("m" is a common, universally-used subdomain for mobile site).

True, the ideal is for your websites to be seamlessly integrated for your visitors, so that a visitor using a mobile device is automatically and instantly redirected to the mobile version of your site. However, there is no law that says you need to take advantage of such technical wizardry. If this is beyond your technical capabilities, there's no reason that your QR Code cannot simply point to the mobile version, wherever it may be.

These are several, single-campaign based Landing Page solutions that can be used to create landing pages for individual campaigns. One point to keep in mind is that your QR Codes may have a shelf life that exceeds your subscription length. Always be cognizant of where users will go, should they encounter your QR Code late in the campaign, or a few months down the line when you've forgotten to pay the bill. Will they arrive someplace friendly? Or receive an error code and think you have no idea what you're doing? Know in advance, and plan accordingly.

- ***Unitaglive.com:*** *I give a full treatment of Unitaglive's other features in the next chapter, but a key feature of their service is that the QR Code generation is a part of the Mobile Marketing process, insofar as the primary thrust of their service is to host Mobile-Optimized Landing Pages and mini-sites to host your responding QR Code-scanning visitors. Payment is on a per-campaign basis, so for a modest sum, a business can host an entire campaign or promotion.*

- **EasyPurl.com**: *Full-spectrum online marketing services; certainly pricey for the novice, but full-featured and robust. Probably only attainable for medium-sized businesses with very ambitious sales goals and strong marketing chops.*
- **Tappinn.com:** *The provider of the mobile Landing Page praised in the previous chapter. Well-conceived pages, full mobile optimization, and QR Code integration is their specialty. Application of most of my recommended Best Practices earns them my own recommendation.*

Form Hosting Services:

Formstack, Wufoo, Survey Monkey, and Jotform are some of the top webform hosting companies. They are brilliantly easy-to-use and offer ready-made forms templates, Mobile-Optimized (or responsive) form pages, low-cost form hosting ($10-20 per month), complete with full analytics support, auto-responder emails, notifier emails, Social Media integration options and a host of other features, to include eCommerce. Some have free trial accounts: Jotform is free for nearly any use… I use it frequently and have never encountered any issue. Wufoo has a free trial account that can host three forms indefinitely (though with some features excluded). Survey Monkey is always free. Use the services several ways:[4]

- *Set up Landing Pages, which are ready and mobile-friendly.*
- *All provide a URL to directly access the form, even without a customized landing page, which is, in essence a landing page.*
- *Most generate simple QR Codes internally to direct to their forms.*
- *All provide website HTML code to export, save and place the form on your site (either to insert into your page, if you are able, or export as an entire complete page).*
- *Most support advanced logic, allowing some form fields or content to be displayed or hidden, based on a visitor's selections.*
- *Both support programmatic API access, and make excellent landing pages for the techie, to capture URL-appended Query Strings into database format.*[5]

Additionally, as of this writing, up-start **Jotform.com** offers free Webform setup similar to FormStack & Woofoo, free of charge for most small-scale use. Bear in mind that free means necessarily bandwidth problems, and so expect UI issues while using it. I wouldn't use it for commercial applications that are extremely vital, but for most low-volume use, it works nicely. Same polished UI as the above two, but with periodic styling and UI errors and hiccups… which have decreased dramatically over the past few months as the service has matured.

A CMS System:

The most popular website Content Management System (CMS), Wordpress, continues to prove popular, stable, and infinitely adaptable. Wordpress provides a content-delivery framework, and works on the Web Server, serving up images, layouts and content on demand. *Themes* (or layouts) can be swapped easily to achieve nearly any website configuration, color scheme, or appearance, and can be downloaded from Wordpress.**org**, or from any number of sources online for free, or purchased for a small fee (themes average $50-60). Use it to build your Landing Page, mini-site or entire website.

- *For the total beginner, use Wordpress.**com** to host your site, and simply point your URL at the http://YourSite.wordpress.com URL using your hosting control panel (or use it as the Landing Page for your QR Code)... for free.*
- *Alternately, another easy option is to host your site at **Wordpress.com** for a fee. This lets them worry about keeping the site active and reliable, but allows you good customization. Use your own domain name if you like.*
- *For those with a bit more web know-how, visit Wordpress.**org** and download the Wordpress CMS system to install it on your own self-hosted site via FTP.*
- *For users of commercial hosting services, such as GoDaddy.com, BlueHost.com, 1and1.com or HostGator.com (and many, many others: most in fact) Wordpress is available for automatic installation through their hosting control dashboards in just a few clicks. Or try out Drupal or Joomla if you like.*

Choose a mobile theme, and you'll be ready for mobile visitors and instantly optimized, permanently. Alternately, choose a ***Responsive*** theme, and your site will automatically adjust based on your user's device, resolution, and screen size, displaying the appropriate size for mobile devices, desktops, tablets, iPads, etc. Even more, Wordpress's user-friendly interface makes building an amazing website a simple matter, even for non-techies and internet novices. Further, their impressive array of free plugins makes even the most complicated web development task simple. Try the following for example plugins:

- *Google Analytics Plugins: Dozens of varieties enable GA tracking for your site visitors with no code editing required. Also, adds GA coding to every page in your site, automating the whole process.*
- *Social Media Plugins: Allow users to sign in and browse your site using their favorite Social Media Accounts, including Google, FaceBook, YouTube, Microsoft, Twitter, LinkedIn, and many, many more. My personal favorite is the OneAll Social Media plugin. OneAll.com. Once users register using the plugin, their contact information is available to you for follow-up contact & marketing.*
- *eCommerce Plugins: Hundreds of eCommerce Plugins will assist you in selling your items online with Paypal Standard, Professional, or even full-featured shopping cart functions, such as Zencart, WooCommerce, JigoShop, and others, as well as payment gateways such as iAuthorize.net.*

- *Mailing List & Membership Plugins: to Manage your website members and even charge for memberships, or restrict content to specific members or membership levels.*
- *Subscription Service Plugins: Got a cult following? Manage them, organize them, and log them in to participate in your forums and community.*
- *Forms Hosting Plugins: Collect your user's information, let them register, take surveys, or do nearly anything.*
- *Search Engine Optimization Plugins: Handle the grunt work of marking up your web pages for Search Engine Optimization, so that your site looks its best and performs well in search engine rankings. No complicated hand-coding of HTML or other website code is necessary; simply add your keywords in the form fields provided.*

Any of these are available for download directly at Wordpress.**org** or installable directly through the Plugins section of the Wordpress dashboard on your site, once the system has been installed.[6]

Basic HTML and CSS Templates

If you have a wee bit of web development savvy, and can hand-edit a bit of HTML, try out one of these sites to download full-featured functional websites, ready to go, without the CMS complexity:

Wix.com - Host websites for free. You'll have their branding on there, but they have an excellent WYSIWYG editor, to make site setup a breeze.

FreeWebsiteTemplates.com - A marketing site for Wix.com, which is around 30% a showcase for their site templates, as well as 70% free downloadable full sites, to place where you wish. Some are quite amazing.

FreeCSSTemplates.org - My favorite of all. The complete package: many, many customizable and free CSS website templates, including many excellent choices for landing pages, many with responsive features. Be sure to check out "Solarize" and "Privy", which are the basis for two of my corporate sites.

Always Remember: Content is King

What did I scan for? Did I waste my time? Was I rewarded for scanning with something useful, interesting, or entertaining? Was I punished with an unreadable page, navigation error, or slow page load? Did I get what was promised, or was I unable to find it? Will I scan again? Answer these questions, and you'll know whether your mobile visitor will be satisfied with the User Experience (UX) of your site and content.

I recently received a Facebook update from a political candidate, whose message was simply, "Like and Share: Help us get to 5 Million Likes." The question was of course, "Why?" What's in it for me? The furor at the polls was over, more than a year ago. The election had passed (and he lost, I'm sorry to say). What was my motivation to Like and Share?

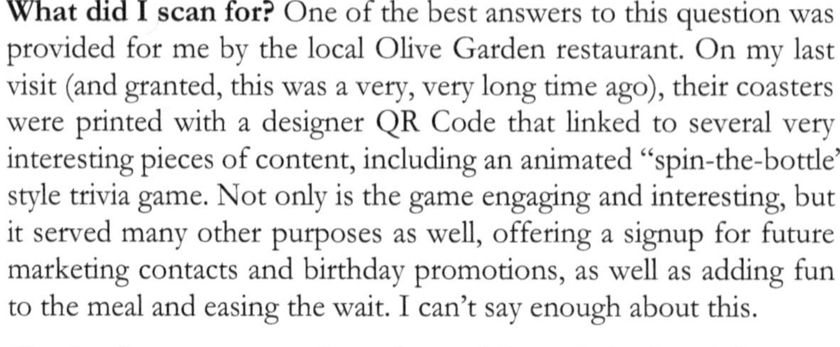

What did I scan for? One of the best answers to this question was provided for me by the local Olive Garden restaurant. On my last visit (and granted, this was a very, very long time ago), their coasters were printed with a designer QR Code that linked to several very interesting pieces of content, including an animated "spin-the-bottle" style trivia game. Not only is the game engaging and interesting, but it served many other purposes as well, offering a signup for future marketing contacts and birthday promotions, as well as adding fun to the meal and easing the wait. I can't say enough about this.

Figure 6 A great QR Code concept

Clearly, the custom-creation of a mobile-optimized mobile game web app is beyond the technical and financial abilities of most businesses. Nonetheless, the spirit of this QR Code application is one that should (and can be) contemplated by all. ***This is meaningful, enjoyable content.*** An excellent, streamlined User Experience. Fun. Have a go.

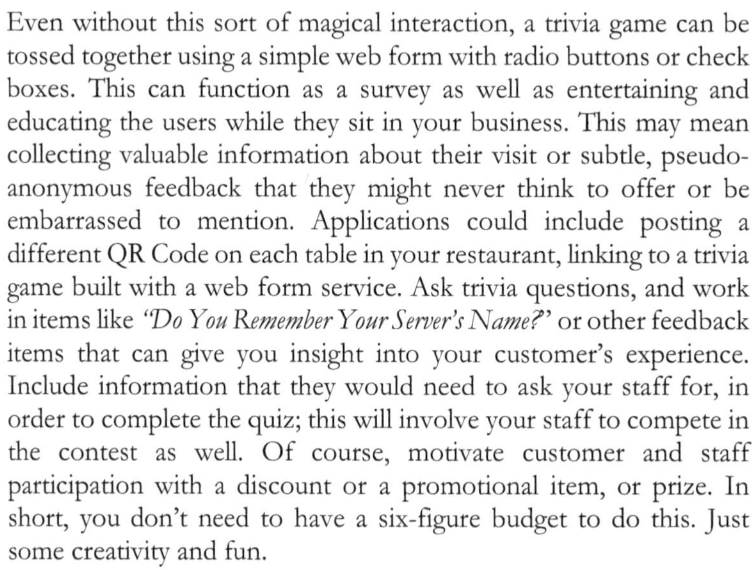

Even without this sort of magical interaction, a trivia game can be tossed together using a simple web form with radio buttons or check boxes. This can function as a survey as well as entertaining and educating the users while they sit in your business. This may mean collecting valuable information about their visit or subtle, pseudo-anonymous feedback that they might never think to offer or be embarrassed to mention. Applications could include posting a different QR Code on each table in your restaurant, linking to a trivia game built with a web form service. Ask trivia questions, and work in items like *"Do You Remember Your Server's Name?"* or other feedback items that can give you insight into your customer's experience. Include information that they would need to ask your staff for, in order to complete the quiz; this will involve your staff to compete in the contest as well. Of course, motivate customer and staff participation with a discount or a promotional item, or prize. In short, you don't need to have a six-figure budget to do this. Just some creativity and fun.

This is what it means to say that Content is King. Content is the bait that gets your customers to your Landing Page, where you can record their contact information, build their interest in your product or brand. You can amuse them with interesting or humorous content that you'd like to see go "viral," or be shared through Social Media channels, interact with them in various ways, or even outright sell them your product.

Don't Be A Selfish Host Online

All too often, marketers and business-owners alike only view their business according to their own needs and desires: *Like my Facebook page. Buy my product. Share my post. Give me your money. Me, me, me.* They throw up a sign, run an advertisement, or stand by the side of the road holding a QR Code and expect that somehow, it will get scanned, and the customers will pour in… just because they want them to, as if their customers and consumer were mere worker bees, with little better to do than spend their online time advocating for a business they hardly recognize. Nothing could be farther from the truth.

Think about it for a moment. Put yourself in your prospective customer's shoes: Why would they want to scan your QR Code? Have you given them an adequate incentive to do so? The same applies to your web page, Landing Page, Social Media pages, and other secondary actions, such as Likes, or even purchases that you'd like them to make. The *why* should be clear in your potential visitor's mind, and it should have value that they can appreciate, and that will make them respond. They aren't going to be randomly curious about your site, and if they are, they certainly won't make the best customers (which is, after all, the end goal).

Give Them a Call to Heed

Now that you've catered to the Mobile Visitor's needs and prepared a place for them that will be mobile-friendly and welcoming, created some content, you just need to tell your prospective QR Code scanner what to do. This is known in advertising and marketing circles as a ***Call to Action*** (C2A). It consists of literally telling the customer precisely what you want them to do, worded as an *imperative*. Meaning, in the second person, literally, "*Do this now.*"

- *Scan HERE to Register for A, B, and C promotion.*
- *Like our Page for a special offer or discount.*
- *Click here for a demonstration of our product.*
- *Scan for a funny video of our owner being attacked by a rabid housecat/vacuum cleaner, a Harlem Shake, our Style video, or one or more of the Spice Girls lip-syncing to Charlie biting his brother's finger.*
- *Scan Here to Download a Free X, Y, or Z.*
- *Scan to visit our contest site to register to win one month's free rent/free product/$500/an iPad/iPhone/iDuJour/gift.*
- *Scan here if you're over 18 years of age, to view a suggestive video of our sexy supermodels making out topless on a basketball court (an accurate C2A for Calvin Klein X's "Uncensored" title).*
- *Scan here to play our spin-the-bottle trivia game, or take our 60-second quiz, for a chance to win our signature dessert, the*

Triple-Fudge Chocolate Nuclear Explosion of Terminal Ecstatic Bliss.

Figure 7

Can't Scan it? Go to: http://eshlepper.com

But Remember: Not Everyone Scans

Statistics and demographics on the QR Code scanning population were quoted earlier. Scanners are a significant portion of those who do respond, *when the response is through a website or Landing Page.* Those who scan, love to scan and prefer it to typing URLs. They'll scan often and readily, and will be ever-present site visitors, and will generally represent a disproportionately and even misleadingly high percentage of your visitors.

But, don't forget that as of today, most people (that means somewhat greater than 50%) haven't yet adopted QR Code scanning at all, let alone as their preferred response vehicle. Those who don't scan, won't. When designing your QR Code, always be aware that to provide only a QR Code, independent of any other means of accessing the online content is a mistake: the majority of your audience is sure to be unwilling or incapable of scanning, so take the time to provide an alternate response method for the non-scanners. A mobile optimized site, responsive site or an entirely different website should be provided for those who have not yet adopted QR Code scanning, and need to type the URL of your Landing Page in order to access it. For these visitors, keep the following in mind:

- ❖ *They will be typing the URL, so lengthy URLs are right out. Using a URL Shortener is vital, unless your landing page is very easy to type and reach directly.*
- ❖ *Avoid mixing upper-case and lower-case letters with numbers, and special characters (&!?) and the query strings you would like to use for response tracking.*[7] *Better keep it simple and rely on your Analytics suite for details.*

Finally, the last reason to include a plain text link: it is entirely possible that your QR Code won't work, or won't work for everyone's device or scanning app. Murphy's Law affects QR Codes just like everything else. Printing errors, poor lighting, glossy paper, poor planning, poor proofreading, an unexpected fold in the middle of the QR Code that damages the ink, or simply *life* can cause your code to fail. When it does, your active QR Code scanners just became hunters and peckers[8] on their Smart Phones; yet another compelling reason to have a plain text URL to accompany all your QR Codes, such as the following:

Several Methods for Doing This

Subdomains of Your Website: Once again, the single, unqualified, best way to add a text only URL for your non-scanning site visitors to access, is to host your Landing Page on a subdomain of your website. Do this through your website's hosting control panel, where you modify *Domain Name Server (DNS)* settings for your website.

Create a new subdomain to host your Landing Page. You can then simply tell your web server where to send traffic that tries to navigate to that page. Hosting your landing page by using a subdomain is the ideal solution for all occasions. It can be re-directed quickly and easily to nearly any URL, and because this takes place at the DNS level (Domain Name Service), it will be just as fast as any other type of access; Thus, this avoids the intermediate stops of using a URL-shortener, and preserves the branding and trust factors discussed elsewhere as strengths of directly-hosted Landing Pages. Examples could include:

- *http://mobile.Eshlepper.com*
- *http://m.Eshlepper.com*
- *http://offer1.Eshlepper.com*
- *http://deals.Eshlepper.com*
- *http://qru.vendorname.com*[9]

Direct Page Navigation: While subdomain hosting is the best option, you may simply want to direct users to your Landing Page by name. In this case, be sure to create landing pages for your site that are easy to type. This is easy to do, and all but automatic, if you're using a CMS. But there is one key problem: your visitors will likely give up at ".com" and fail to type the whole URL, ending up on your home page, which is not exactly what you necessarily want, if you directed them there for a specific reason or promotion. One of the key strengths of QR Codes is that they are infallible, when done right, and there is no human error to intervene.[10] Always be sure to keep it short: if they're typing, don't ask them to type forever. They won't.

- *http://www.Eshlepper.com/offer1 (note no file extension… in this case, "offer1" is the directory, and your destination is an "index.html" file in this directory.*
- *Or by actual filename: "offer#1.html" (punctuation is best avoided as difficult to type, as well as capital letters or look-alike letters, which will mess things up in a filename)*
- *http://www.Eshlepper.com/offer2*
- *actual filename: "offer2.html"*

Using a Public URL-Shortening Service: A URL Shortener is another way to create an easily typed, keyboard-friendly short URL for your non-scanning visitors to type. You will necessarily sacrifice some the branding benefits of self-hosting your site, as the primary URL displayed will be that of the URL shortener service. Nevertheless, some URL shorteners, most notably Bit.ly, are popular and reputable services that are trusted by major websites, like Twitter & Facebook, and used by large companies everywhere… and can be linked to your own domain name to use your site like Bit.ly… again, with some technical configuration required.

Bit.ly even allows users to re-name the short URLs as they please (provided the names are not taken, which may take some trial and error... and keep in mind you can only have around 5 custom-named links, or each successive one will un-name a previous one… a royally frustrating scenario, and something done with no notice to the user). A login is required to re-name your "Bitmarks," but once a Bit.ly account is created, all your bitmarks will be kept organized.

```
http://bit.ly/GIlIIdf4r
(ugly, and impossible to type due to look-alike
letters) becomes…
http://bit.ly/UltimateQRs
```

Use a Vanity URL Shortener: In later chapters, I describe the installation of a URL Shortener directly on your own site, which enables better branding for your site, and all sorts of other uses. Some key points that should be mentioned about all of these methods are as follows:

- ✓ *Beware of look-alike letters, such as q/g, i/j, l/1/I, m/rn, etc, which could look nearly identical, depending on the font used, including "Calibri", which I've used for the bulleted lists herein. Can you tell which of the above is an l and which is an 1? or is it an I?). If there's any ambiguity, change the link so that it's clear to your visitors; if they can't read it, they can't type it. They won't try hard.*
- ✓ *Also, while website domain and subdomain URLs are not case sensitive, that is, they don't discriminate between upper- and lowercase letters. However, webpage filenames usually are case sensitive, and so are URL-shortened keywords.*
- ✓ *Bear in mind that your visitors will likely have difficulty capitalizing some letters, and will no doubt try to type in all-lowercase letters, which will get them to the wrong place. To get around this, use lowercase letters exclusively wherever possible.*

Best Practices

See the Chapter on *Best Practices* for the brief, definitive listing of all these recommended guidelines, as well as others from the rest of this book.

---

[1] *That's only the beginning of the information available; a tiny example. The same information shows that several pages of the site bleed visitors like a sieve. Upon further investigation, loading problems were discovered, etc.*

[2] *GoDaddy's DudaMobile integration was so easy and amazing that it had me giggling with glee (usually I just gripe). However, one problem I encountered was that in my shared hosting account, only one mobile website could be configured, and by default this was for the "main account." All 13 of my sites redirected mobile users to the same mobile site, so I had to disable it. Not good. For shared hosting accounts, ie, hosting more than one website in the same space, multiple accounts will be necessary.*

[3] *Mofuse was the service used by "The Flyer" in the example shown. Their bill went unpaid, which is a good reason to use a service with a free option, even if you need to tolerate their logo. If you miss your payment, or change the credit card you use for billing, or any of a million reasons, you don't want your mobile site to evaporate. Rather, defaulting to the free option will at least keep your visitors directing to the right page.*

[4] *Wufoo tends to be a bit more user-friendly for the casual user, and there are differences in the integrations possible, as these companies are direct competitors, each favoring some vendors over others. My preference for Formstack stems from several factors: Far better control automatically configuring integrations, ability to export & share forms between accounts, details of the API, specific integrations available, etc.*

[5] *See chapter on Advanced Strategies for more on Query Strings.*

[6] *The various Wordpress installation options will allow varied levels of Plugin use and functionality, as well as customizability. For best results, self-host on your own web server or host for a small yearly fee with Wordpress.com. Note that the tagline "Proudly Powered By Wordpress" cannot be*

---

eliminated when your site is hosted with Wordpress, whether free or with a paid subscription. Removing their branding requires hand-editing of your source files, something not to be attempted by the novice or the faint of heart. As proud as I am to be powered by Wordpress, the reference isn't always welcome.

[7] *None of these can be typed easily by a mobile user or even by most desktop users. Ask me where to find a #-symbol on a Blackberry keyboard, or if I know the complex combination of keystrokes necessary to complete the task. So, for those like me who are disposed to advanced URL-appended data and tracking information, you'll have to give that up for those who type the URL directly, or use a shortener.*

[8] *Hunting & Pecking: n. The technique employed by two-finger typists. Awkward typing.*

[9] *When purchasing a hosted Landing Page solution from a vendor, usually your link will be directed to a subdomain of theirs, branded for you. This is sub-optimal, but is the next-best solution to hosting it yourself.*

[10] *For an interesting, and practical variation, combine subdomain hosting with direct navigation hosting, by creating a direct page for the visitor landing page, and code that into the QR Code (it doesn't matter if it's hard to type, since the QR Code will be processed automatically). Then, set up your subdomain with nothing on it, but simply redirected to your landing page in your DNS settings. That way, QR Code scanners will go directly to the right location, and URL-typers will see a pretty URL that is easy to type. Be sure to slap a query string on one or both to differentiate them. Then, you'll see who's scanning and who's typing.*

13. Getting Fancy

We've covered the basics for QR Code generators and tools, as well as theory and essential points for getting the QR Code usage right. Now, it's time to raise the bar in the appearance department. The plain black and white QR Codes that you've seen everywhere are really only the most basic level of this art. And, given what's out there, it hardly seems like much effort at all.

Remember that Denso-Wave's QR Codes were originally designed as data-intensive bar codes to track parts and production in Toyota's plants: purely industrial applications. As such, only function, high-speed readability and cheap generation matter in this environment; function is paramount, and form is irrelevant, adding needless expense.

QR Codes: Ugly No Longer

But, now that QR Codes have left the factory, and are running loose on the street, figuring prominently in marketing messages for every brand imaginable, it's fitting that they clean up their act and dress the part. The Spartan, purely utilitarian look is great for a post-industrial *Dada* statement. But, for the rest of the world, style is vital. And in a marketing message? Come on! In fact, the very human soul cries out for creativity and artistic expression… or at least a splash of color.

Using color is one of my identified Best Practices. One would think it obvious, but it needs to be mentioned. ***Use color***. The mere fact that the majority of QR Code users do not employ color of any sort is perplexing, and presents a great opportunity to easily distinguish yourself from the pack. Most readers of these lines are probably shocked that colors are possible… and easily output by most generators, since they may have never seen a colorful one. For whatever reason, color has yet to catch on in any broad and observable way, at least in the American marketplace, which is why the style leader is a French company.

I Feel Pretty... Oh, So Pretty...

For practical purposes, softening the edges creates inviting, touchable technology that invites interest, inquiry, curiosity, and interaction. This is a core value of the marketing business, creating a positive response. The below tools bring precisely this to the table. Seize the opportunity to use basic color at a minimum, for all QR Codes, wherever feasible, or get even more bang for the buck by using the advanced features of these sites:

QRstuff.com[1] - My own long-time choice for QR Code creation and archiving, with a simple and straightforward interface. Supports at least 20 QR Code data storage formats, including vCard, MeCard, Phone number, URL, etc. Virtually unlimited length with their built-in option using their *Qrs.ly* URL shortener as you create, using their QRs.ly shortener.

My own business applications call for keeping track of hundreds or even batches of tens of thousands of one-off QR codes in custom colors for client campaigns, and their archiving feature keeps it all organized. I also have the need to quickly change the destination URLs for the short codes, so QRStuff is top-notch. The additional functionality for bulk uploads makes generating tens of thousands of unique QR Codes a snap. A subscription purchase enables tracking and metrics, click-through statistics, and all the bells and whistles, including infographics and report export functions for analysis (some were used throughout this book). Further, an additional for-fee service enables extremely high-volume uploads for a reasonable cost on an as-needed basis. The downside is the same as with any professional option: to take advantage of many of these features, a significant facility with data manipulation is needed, as the uploads must be properly formatted. Some tools to assist are available on the companion website for this book, for download. Foreground color is the only "fancy" option. This is a cost-effective, all-business service to get big jobs done. Their staff is very helpful, and has answered questions very quickly, before and during work on this book.

Figure 8 QR Hacker's QR Codes

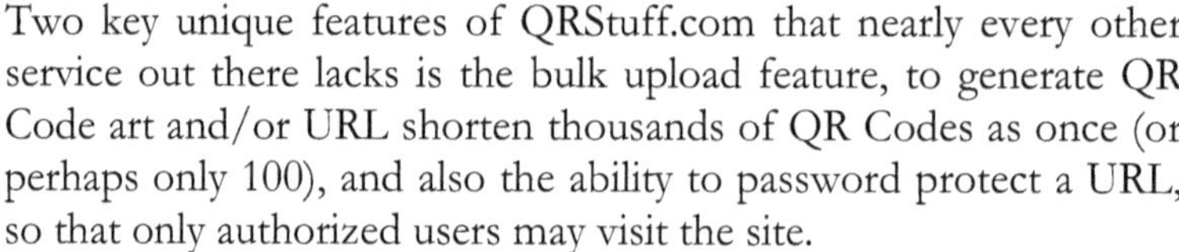

Two key unique features of QRStuff.com that nearly every other service out there lacks is the bulk upload feature, to generate QR Code art and/or URL shorten thousands of QR Codes as once (or perhaps only 100), and also the ability to password protect a URL, so that only authorized users may visit the site.

UnitagLive.com The QR Code generator par excellence for luscious edit-free Designer QR Codes with almost unlimited customizable options, at no charge as of this writing to produce one-off QR Codes, although I have encountered the need to be patient, as the site frequently has trouble with bandwidth. All examples on this page are unaltered QR Codes output from the site, for free, no registration required. Varied shapes for corner blocks and centers, dots, fluid shapes and smoothly-flowing soft-edged data areas, as well as alternate background colors and gradients, drop shadows (be really careful with that one) and even logo incorporation, all to play with on a one-off basis for free. With the paid service, users can also enjoy significant tracking and metrics options, archiving, dynamic codes (ie, changeable destination page), landing page hosting, and other features.

Figure 9 Unitag's QR Codes

This service stands out two key areas: First, the focus on building a mobile mini-site as a QR Code Landing Page. Second, the rich interface enables some of the most complicated and beautiful QR Codes to be generated. Very impressive, although for high volumes of QR Codes, it can get pricey. Unitag's staff is also very helpful, personally responding to requests for assistance via email and working to help make best use of their service, including offering me a free credit to play with the API and get it right. Each of the above six QR Codes was created directly from UnitagLive's site, with no re-touching or hand editing whatsoever. If you're reading the black & white version of this book and are curious what they look like in color, visit http://eshlepper.com/, as each of them is used in the site background image.

QrHacker.com - With a unique user interface and free-user features that are above average, QrHacker.com offers some unique and unusual options found in few other places: adjust the roundness of the pixels for a less stark look, background color (or image) as well as foreground color (or image), and even a WYSIWYG (What-You-See-Is-What-You-Get) option to draw on your QR Code, pixel by pixel, which is how I created the adorable smiley-face. This is a great option for users who want to incorporate some high-end hand-made QR Code features, without advanced image processing software or skills. Surprise feature? As you draw on the QR Code, it displays a running display of how close you get to modifying the QR Code beyond readability, a very nice touch and a unique one I've seen nowhere else. I recommend that all readers who wish to customize their QR Codes visit, just for that feature alone, to get a feel for what's simply *too much.*

BeQRious.com - Typical of most QR Code generation service websites. Boasts an astonishing array of options, but requires a $5/month fee for nearly all functions. For free users, only the most basic color selection is allowed above. The paid service unlocks substantial options of use for the professional marketer, including the usual metrics & click-through statistics. Yet another example of an easy site to use to make dramatic, colored QR Codes. Where's all the color, folks?

Figure 10 BeQRious

And That's Not All...

These are hardly the only sites online offering QR Code generation services, but are rather merely a quick sampling of a broad spectrum of options. Most sites are roughly the same, but many sites out there have at least one entirely unique feature that will impress you.

[1] *QRStuff.com has made a tentative offer to link to this book online, from their site, which obviously may or may not have monetary value for the author, and may or may not ultimately happen. The author's recommendation and enthusiasm for this service is based purely on the service's merits and pre-dates said offer.*

14. Bending the Rules

One of the top criticisms of QR Codes is their stark, industrial appearance. While this high-tech look is indeed a reason for the popularity of QR Codes as well, it can be argued that the black & white QR Code is simply too Spartan. I have to agree. And, depending on placement and use, it may not present itself as a cohesive part of the marketing message at all. Rather, it could be easily perceived as merely another bar code. For example, on product packaging, or shipping containers, etc, it might be dismissed as simply another random extraneous barcode. Consumers have been ignoring barcodes for years; what's to tell them that this barcode is *for them specifically*.

For example, many shippers use varied technologies to track shipments, including Dot Code and Datamatrix codes, which are in widespread use with companies such as UPS for parcel tracking. In the foregoing section, we explored several excellent sites for adding color and style to your QR Codes.

Why Stop at Designer QR Codes?

Beyond these options, lies the realm of the pure art QR Code, that one-off artistic wonder that simply cannot be computer-generated or replicated. At the end of the chapter are examples of my own humble (though worthy) custom QR Codes, and hundreds more can be found online. While these custom QR Codes were painstakingly created with image editing software, similar and even more impressive QR Codes can be made by any number of companies online, who will (for a fee) create you a truly one-of-a-kind QR Code.

- *http://www.CustomQRCodes.com/custom-qr-codes-gallery*
- *http://BeQRious.com/custom-qr-codes*

There is certainly no shortage of sites available and ready to create your custom, Designer QR Code for you for a fee. But, if you're in business for yourself, more likely this is an expense that you can't seriously consider. But, consider this: It is actually quite easy to edit your own QR Codes using any image editing software, ranging from Adobe Photoshop & Illustrator, or Microsoft Paint & Apple Image Preview, or even Microsoft Word or Publisher.

In fact, all of the designer QR Codes I've created (for this book, and in) were done using Apple's on-board Image Preview, which is so basic that it isn't really even considered image editing software. Here's how to do this:

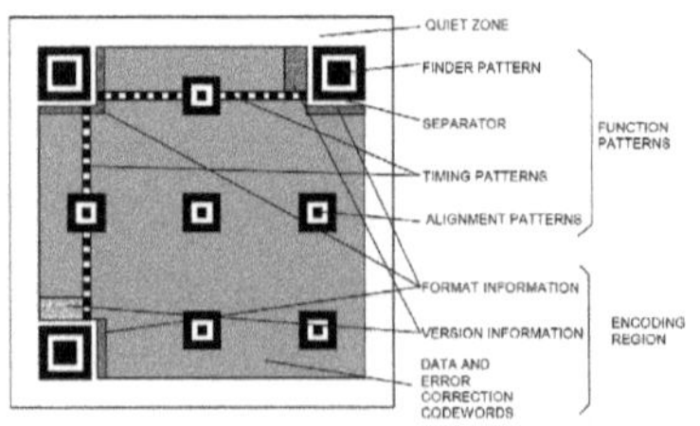

Figure 11 Image Source: ISO 18004: QR Code 2005 www.iso.org

First, Get Clear on Structure:

Much information on the QR Code data coding structure in earlier chapters was omitted as unnecessary to the process of creating basic QR Codes. I dismissed it, as prior to this point, all QR Code generation has been recommended using generators and keeping it by the book. However, if you're going to set about radically customizing your QR Codes, the time has come to take just a few moments to consider the underlying data structure, if only to avoid ruining your QR Code and making it unworkable.

QR Code technology is very robust, and has many built-in features to ensure scanning under most conditions, including:

- *Built-in discriminator data to allow code recognition.*
- *Built-in data & formatting validation areas to verify valid coding.*
- *Automatic orientation detection (for accurate up-side-down scans)*
- *Built-in redundant data (to ensure correct scanning, even when the QR Code is partially obscured, damaged, or has missing ink)*

Ground Rules for Breaking QR Codes

This makes QR Codes quite quick & easy to scan under most conditions, even when misused. But, as with any kind of interaction with technology, there are always some ground rules and limitations that must be heeded, in order for them to function properly. The best policy to follow is always to display QR Codes properly. Unfortunately, that's not much fun, and since we've decided to break them, here are the rules for the best results; always be sure to keep the following limitations in mind.

Figure 12 Finder Patterns

The Importance of the Finder Pattern

Commonly referred to the 'eyes' of the QR Code, are squares within squares, located at three corners of the QR Code. These are the first basic features that QR Scanning apps look for when trying to find and read a QR Code. *Without one or more of the finder squares, the QR Code will be impossible to read.* The Finder Pattern is indicated in gray here, and one is entirely missing from the QR Code at right. Note that it simply cannot be scanned. This applies, whether the Finder Pattern is entirely missing, or if it is simply blocked in some way, perhaps by artwork that crowds or overlaps it, or if the center eye is missing. No go.

Figure 13 Orientation Patterns

The Orientation Pattern

The Orientation Pattern is the other clearly identifiable feature of a QR Code that can be seen by the untrained eye. It is a fourth, mini finder square situated at the lower right of the QR Code[1], and is shown in this next diagram, in gray for emphasis, and also completely missing. Obstructing or removing the orientation pattern, to include the black box that encloses it, will result in an unscannable QR Code. It is interesting to note that the simplest QR Code (Called "Version 1") lacks any orientation pattern. Note that as the data load climbs (ie, the length of the URL or other data stored), more "modules" and orientation patterns are added by the generator.

The 'Quiet Zone' of the QR Code

The Quiet Zone is the space around the QR Code. In order for the QR Code to be read properly, the scanner application must be able to discern the Finder Pattern from the surrounding art, text & images that are near the QR Code. Usually, this isn't an issue, and the QR Code can be located well away from any other elements on the page, without too much difficulty. In fact, using a generated QR Code as-is will generally ensure good operation, since every generator includes the requisite Quiet Zone. However, strictly locating the QR Code on a white background, distinct from other elements can be very limiting, specifically on documents with a background color, or when it is desirable to break up the starkness of the QR Code by bringing it closer to other elements, or even overlaying and blending it with other elements.

Officially, the recommended Quiet Zone is equivalent to the width of the center eye of the three Finder Patterns, as indicated above at left by the dashed line. However, for practical purposes, in most applications of QR Codes, this can be reduced to the width of a single QR Code pixel unit (above, center) and the QR Code will remain fully readable for most scanning apps. In fact, in testing, I've had occasional good results with zero Quiet Zone, as long as no art encroached *into* the Finder Patterns. But that's the exceptional case. Definitely be sure to stick to at least a reasonable quiet zone of several QR Code pixel units, perhaps 3 or more.

Timing, Version and Formatting Areas

As indicated in the preceding diagram labeling the features of the QR Code, these areas also contain vital information about the QR Code and how it should be deciphered. So, they are best preserved, as is. The result of covering these areas (with a logo, for example) can be more subtle and unpredictable than the results of tampering with the Quiet Zone, Finder and Alignment Patterns, usually having a less profound effect, ranging from little to no effect, but potentially resulting in a longer scan time, as the application struggles to figure it out. This is definitely not good. Remember, your potential site visitors are in a rush and fickle. If they're willing to scan, be ready to deliver.

Mind Your Foreground/Background Contrast:

One exception to my rule that using a commercial QR Code generator is safe, is in the area of contrast. A QR Code Generator that allows color selection will generally allow you to select at least the foreground (dark space color) and perhaps even the background (white space) color. There are limits to how light a QR Code can be before it is rendered unreadable. You could very easily set the colors too similar in contrast, and end up with a bad QR Code.

The higher the contrast, the better. But, of course, to stick with the highest contrast, we'd be stuck with black and white, the highest contrast there is. I always recommend color, so in using colors, it's important to try to stick to dark colors to the extent possible. Very light grays or any light color, such as yellow, or pastels, will impact the contrast and make QR Codes difficult to scan, such as these examples. Bear in mind that some colors may see darker to the human eye than a camera, for example, the way highlighters of many varieties and colors are invisible to photocopiers, while they may seem quite dark or bright in color. Keep in mind that colors may not necessarily be equivalent to darkness.

It's best to keep the foreground color as dark as possible. Above are some samples of shades to demonstrate how readability is affected by contrast. I have yet to scan the right-most QR Code, but the second-lowest contrast works fine with several applications, so this issue can be avoided in most cases. The technology is robust, and the scanning applications are very capable. Also note that I am speaking from attempts to scan these on screen. QR Codes are far easier to scan from paper, unless the paper is colored. In this case, some testing will be necessary. I've had acceptable results from all four on paper, but unless there's a terribly pressing reason you want the QR Code all but invisible, stick to the highest contrast you can use.

Figure 14:

Contrast variations.

Background Contrast/Transparency

Most generators will use white for the background for nearly every QR Code application, but a few generators allow a custom background color selection. This should be used judiciously, since darkening the background color has the same net effect as lightening the foreground color. Stick with the lightest colors. Many QR Code generators also allow download of the QR Code image with a transparent (or alpha) background, which allows anything behind the QR Code to show through the white space. This can be a great feature for allowing the QR Code to be easily integrated into other artwork, to help it appear as a fluid part of the rest of your marketing message. But, it also allows the QR Code to be accidentally placed on too dark a background, resulting in an unreadable QR Code due to low contrast.

QR Code Print Method

Most readers will probably print their QR Codes on their home laser or inkjet on the appropriate paper, which is great. In fact, everything is always great when QR Codes are a large size and unedited on white paper.

But some readers may print their QR Codes (along with the materials they are attached to) in small batches with a commercial digital printer. Note that commercial printers will often use a number of different processes to print a single piece, and really only a professional would be able to tell the difference. One thing to watch out for is a high-speed commercial inkjet printer commonly used to "spray" the address information onto mailers. The precision and resolution of this type of printer is not adequate for QR Codes. This is the fate that befalls many QR Codes I receive in the mail: they're just ever so slightly too blurry to scan.

So, for those who outsource their print needs, I offer this advice:

1. *Inquire about the print process that will be used to print your QR Codes. Digital laser is always great. But, if the QR Codes will be "sprayed on" by an Inkjet (particularly Variable QR Codes printed uniquely from a database file or spreadsheet at the same time as the items are addressed), it will no doubt be done just barely too fast, and the ink left too wet, and cause bad results. Several skilled printers I've worked with will either claim that the Inkjet cannot print QR Codes, warn that it's suboptimal, or refuse to do it by inkjet.*
2. *If inkjet is the only option, take the extra step to decrease the error correction[2]. You won't need it.*
3. *Decrease the data load and version (see below for examples). A simpler QR Code means lower resolution, and fewer, larger QR Code pixel units. Shorten the URLs if you have to, in bulk if necessary.*
4. *Print the darned thing larger. Sometimes, the realization that there's a problem strikes too late in the game to re-adjust or go back to the drawing board, re-work art, data, etc. In that case, give thought to increasing the QR Code size itself. Larger will always be more easily scanned.*
5. *When in doubt, don't trust the QR Code to an inferior print method via variable data on the printing press. You can always hedge against any errors by incorporating the QR Code into the mailer art itself, for a no-error solution that also opens up the door to more color and customization options. Most variable data (comes in Henry Ford's palette: "You can have it in any color you like, as long as it's black."*

Bear in mind that none of this applies to the home printer, or someone who runs out to the copy store for basic digital color or black & white copies. These print processes will be slow and precise, and universally produce good results.

Special Effects and Flourishes

Note also that effects generated by the QR Code generators, for example, UnitagLive's shadow effect, can be as bad as a dark background. A slight shadow looks fantastic, but dramatically impacts the ease of scanning. A dark one can make the QR Code impossible to scan. **Use due diligence: just because the generator allows it as an option, this doesn't necessarily make it a good idea.**

*A Brief, NON-Technical Note on Color Spaces

Without getting *too* technical, it also should be noted that printed items use a different color system than colors displayed on a screen. Computer monitors and displays use RGB color: **R**ed, **G**reen, and **B**lue lights that vary and combine to make all the colors you see. In a printer (whether a commercial printer or your home laser or inkjet printer), **C**yan (Blue), **M**agenta, **Y**ellow, and Blac**K** ink or toner is used to create *similar* colors. Most laymen won't have any idea what the difference is, and will never have noticed one. And usually, there won't be a discernable difference. But, printers, photographers, and graphic designers… or really, really picky people know that these two systems result in two totally different color spectrums that can be produced: what are called "color gamuts." A screen can approximate nearly any color imaginable. On paper, though, frequently, you may encounter a situation where a color appears dramatically different in print because a printer simply cannot reproduce the richness or shade of a color as displayed on screen. Usually, in most applications, *close* is good enough. But, because QR Codes can be sensitive to contrast, be aware that what you see… is NOT necessarily what you get. Always test a printed copy. Generally, QR Codes will always scan better live from paper than from a screen, but you may encounter color combinations that surprise. So, test, test, test.

QR Code Data Density

Another vitally important factor to keep in mind when creating QR Codes is to keep the data density low. A QR Code, as we've noted earlier can be used to code as many as 4,296 characters of alphanumeric text (letters & numbers). Be advised: This limit is <u>theoretical</u> and reflects the maximum data that can possibly be stored in the QR Code matrix, which always greatly exceeds the capabilities of the scanning app or Smart Phone camera. It also means that the QR Code will need to be displayed far larger than you would ever want to display it, in order for a scanning application to reliably decipher it. These examples give you an idea of how QR Codes progress from low data density to high data density, with the number of characters encoded given. Note that there is a break between the

8th and 9th sample: I jumped to the extreme situations. But really, these aren't as bad as it can get.

Sample Matrix Sizes vs. Data Content: (Maximum Data Shown).

Remember that as the quantity of stored data grows, the complexity of the QR Code increases automatically as well, quickly making them more and more difficult to scan. Keep the character count down to only a single URL length, perhaps 20-30 characters at most, for the simplest, most user-friendly QR Codes. There are also additional key points to consider about data density:

At the fixed points where the QR Code matrix grows, more Alignment Patterns are added automatically by the generator. Each of these is governed by the same rule mentioned earlier: Don't obscure them. Thus, by not keeping the data load to a minimum, and allowing your matrix size to get too large, soon the QR Codes will have too many sensitive areas that require protecting, meaning that you won't have as many viable customization options, since nearly anything you do to decorate the QR Code will block at least one of the many Alignment Patterns. Note in the diagram above that there are 0, 1, 1, 1, 1, 1, 6, 6, 6, 6, 13, and finally 22 individual Alignment Patterns (you can count them yourself), potentially removing any potential for any customizations. Where could they fit?

Note also that the Version 1 QR Code (top left) as no Alignment Pattern, so if the data load can be kept VERY low, to a simple shortened URL, it's possible to have NO orientation patterns, opening up even more customization options. Of course, this is nearly impossible, unless one secures an extremely short URL to host content, such as *Eshlepper.com.* Some generators don't allow Version 1 encoding, and start out at Version 2 (one Alignment Pattern). QRstuff.com, for example, will allow Version1 Encoding.

For Best Results

QR Codes are best looking and best scanning at the lowest matrix resolutions. Work hard to keep the data content to the 21x21 or 25x25 matrix (so-called QR Code Versions 1 & 2), by keeping them less than 30 encoded letters and numbers long. The table below demonstrates the increase in resolution of the QR Code matrix size as the quantity of data increases.

But, rarely is it necessary to store more than a simple URL or web address in a QR Code, and only for more advanced tracking applications. If there is simply no way to trim the information you need to store in the QR Code, review the next chapter on URL Shortening, which is often a necessary companion to such QR Code applications. This enables substantial additional data to be attached to the URL encoded in the QR Code, without increasing the matrix size. This is possible because the data is pre-formatted and stored elsewhere, and only a short reference link to the data is stored in the QR Code matrix itself.

QR Code Size

Sample Matrix Sizes vs. URL Length (and Error Correction)					
Version	Code Size WidthxHeight:	Low EC:	Medium EC:	Quality EC:	High EC:
1	21x21 Squares	25	20	16	10
2	25x25 Squares	47	38	29	20
3	29x29 Squares	77	61	47	35
4	33x33 Squares	114	90	67	50
5	37x37 Squares	154	122	87	64
6	41x41 Squares	195	154	108	84
7	45x45 Squares	224	178	125	93
8	49x49 Squares	279	221	157	122
9	53x53 Squares	335	262	189	143
10	57x57 Squares	395	311	221	174

Sample QR Code Matrix Sizes (color indicates safe, suspect & excessive data density)

No discussion of QR Code resolution and data density can be done without talking about the most obvious influencer of resolution: the actual size of the QR Code. You can experiment for weeks with scanning the typical QR Code and come to the same conclusion that Microsoft's Tag folks came up with: A QR Code size should be at least 1/7th the expected scan distance. That means, for a QR Code on a mailer that one holds in their hand to scan, at a distance of say, 5 inches, a ¾" QR Code is just fine. Less is not so good. Closer than ~4 inches at the autofocus capability of the device breaks down: So you can't simply say, "they'll move closer." There is only so close they can get.

So, ¾" to 1" in size is the ideal. At 1-inch they look a bit on the large size. Larger is unnecessary.

But, for the sake of argument, note that scans can be possible, even at ridiculously small sizes. I once published one type of QR Code that was specifically NOT designed to be scanned by consumers, but was designed to be as small and discrete as possible, for the business owners to scan as their coupons were returned as a rudimentary way to track response without collecting the coupons, hording them, losing them, or forgetting about them.

This is also why billboard QR Codes are so ill-advised: At a scan distance of 300 feet, say for a pedestrian near a billboard, the requisite ideal QR Code size is… 40+ feet across. Typical billboard sizes are 14'x48' and 10'x36. Do the math. It would be an unusual billboard that would work. More on that later.

QR Code Outline Specification

Symbol size	21 × 21 - 177 × 177 modules (size grows by 4 modules/side)	
Type & Amount of Data (Mixed use is possible.)	Numeric	Max. 7,089 characters
	Alphanumeric	Max. 4,296 characters
	8-bit bytes (binary)	Max. 2,953 characters
	Kanji	Max. 1,817 characters
Error correction (data restoration)	Level L	Approx. 7% of codewords can be restored.
	Level M	Approx. 15% of codewords can be restored.
	Level Q	Approx. 25% of codewords can be restored.
	Level H	Approx. 30% of codewords can be restored.
Structured append	Max. 16 symbols (printing in a narrow area etc.)	

Redundancy and Error Correction

One of the most unique features of the QR Code, and one that has had so little of its potential unlocked, is the concept of error correction. QR Codes got their start in the Toyota automobile plants, and so it is geared for industrial applications. This means that it had to be designed to be highly robust and reliable, working in hot, dirty, high-traffic environments, potentially outdoors, and had to keep working, as stopping to replace them costs time and money. Thus, they were designed to be able to tolerate wear and tear, and even outright damage and missing ink, and keep performing reliably and returning the correct data, failing gracefully for as long as possible. Time, after all, is money.

Source: DENSO-WAVE INCORPORATED, www.denso-wave.com

The chart above shows the maximum data storage based on text encoding and error correction level. QR Code error correction has four levels: **L**ow, **M**edium, **Q**uartile, and **H**igh, and are designated by the initial letters for the same. Essentially, as can be seen from the chart, a level of error correction of "High" preserves the readability of a QR Code, even when 30% of the data areas are missing or corrupted, a true asset when used in a high-traffic area, long-term installation, or for when precise reading is essential.

Today's marketing and consumer uses of QR Codes generally give us little reason to be concerned about wear & tear or long-term reliability. More often than not, they are kept safe, dry, and sheltered. They are further, more often than not, printed on something disposable, which won't be around long enough to endure much abuse. Further, they aren't so very high-risk. On occasion, if a QR Code scan goes awry, for a single consumer with an odd app in suboptimal light, it won't be the end of the world. An entire assembly line won't be stopped dead for an hour while a robot re-attempts a QR Code scan in vain 20,000 times in a row. So, we don't really need the error correction of a QR Code to guard against damage.

But, since we have it anyway, we can use the error correction to deliberately damage our QR Codes. More to the point, this preserves readability when you deliberately damage your QR Codes, remove some of the code or partially block it with logos or artistic elements.

Enter the Designer QR Code

I write *damaged* facetiously. Custom QR Codes have been called many things: "Artistically-Compromised" QR Codes, "Designer QR Codes" and many others. But, the meaning is clear: These are not QR Codes that were produced mechanically by a generator, but were rather the product of some degree of skill and creativity, with a bit of sacrifice made in the area of pure efficiency, in favor of artistic and design considerations.

Much can be done with QR Code generators such as UnitagLive.com's generator, which is responsible for the many amazing QR Codes featured in the previous chapter on 'Getting Fancy', and shown again above. The capabilities of this generator should be as much as anyone could ever need, it even allows for a small (make that *miniscule)* logo to be uploaded and placed in the center of the QR Code[3].

Who could ask for more? And yet, you're still reading. Many would like to take the capabilities of QR Codes and combine them with amazing color and contrast, and also add-in their own logo or other items. Due to the ability of the QR Code to store up to 30% redundant information, artistic overlays of all types become possible. Not only can the QR Code be functional, but it can be attractive, re-enforce your brand's identity, and also morph itself into various shapes to suit your needs. It need not be obtrusive, but can be an entirely fluid part of your company's marketing message, including your logo, theme, or even your face.

All that's necessary is the most basic of image editing software tools. Adobe Photoshop or Illustrator are great and truly helpful, but the learning curve can be quite high to accomplish anything in Photoshop… let alone Illustrator. When I wrote the first edition, I had zero such talents, my only digital art experience being Microsoft Paint. In the two years since then, I've become a Photoshop wizard. I can definitely say that Photoshop will make this job a thousand times easier and more effective, and so I've included a few Photoshop-specific tips. But it isn't necessary. All of my original suggestions are still possible for almost anyone, using nothing more than the simplest tools: Microsoft Paint, Mac Image Preview, or any simple image editor.

Even Microsoft Paint or Apple's Preview image viewer have sufficient power to create all of these Designer QR Codes. Now, some are more difficult that others, granted, but all are well within the abilities of nearly anyone. It just takes the desire and a bit of effort.

How These QR Codes Were Made:

There really isn't space to run down every possible step involved in customizing QR Codes like these; it's beyond the scope of this book. However, here are a few quick notes on how some very basic techniques were employed to create some of the QR Codes herein, in order of least to most complicated and technically demanding. However if ANY of the QR Code data area will be covered or blocked by additions, it is vitally important that the QR Code be encoded from the start using a generator that allows a custom error correction setting. Choose the highest error correction, "H" for

"High." This will allow the best readability, and cover a host of mistakes. And of course, as always, with any hand-editing, take a moment to blow up your image to 4x normal size: this one trick will always allow you to work with a much steadier hand, and hide mistakes better.

Automotive Client QR Codes:

These QR Codes were created on behalf of clients, in the course of marketing campaigns, and were the easiest of all to create. Actually, they took just a few minutes. The center version is simply a red QR Code generated at QRStuff.com: not much difficulty there. The other two utilized basic options at UnitagLive.com. The client's logo was added over the QR Code after generation. Unitag's interface will only add a tiny logo automatically, which is rarely enough… but if you want to skirt the image editing entirely, go for it. You'll achieve the best results in that case with a wide, narrow logo like that at left.

The only thing needed is a logo with a transparent background; a white background will block more of the QR Code data than is absolutely necessary. Striking a balance with logo size is a tight-rope act. You'll always want the logo larger than is possible. Such is life. Both of these logos at right are too large. The one at left is precisely right, and done to excellent effect.

Some trial-and-error is necessary, so save frequently. Start out with a very small logo, and slowly UNDO and increase the size, double-checking by scanning the QR Code to be sure that it still scans. Adobe Photoshop, or any image editing software that permits saving images in separate layers will speed this up tremendously. Refer back to the diagram earlier in this chapter that identifies the QR Code features that should not be obscured.

Also a UnitagLive.com code, using the 'Sieve' pattern, as well as specifying white for the corner eyes. Custom QR Code corner 'eyes', or Finder Patterns with the company logo were added, as well as the large logo at center. This was also very easy to do. It can be thrown together reliably by a novice in just a few minutes.

Toolbox QR Code.

This was another very easy effect to create. First, I found an image for my company's toolbox theme. Next, created a QR Code in a matching color. After cutting out part of the QR Code, I distorted the QR Code by compressing it, to give it a more squat, wider look, much like a toolbox. Stretching is not often seen with QR Codes, but they will tolerate significant distortion, and in the worst case, they can simply be scanned at an oblique angle to make them appear normal. This provides ample opportunity for oddly-placed QR Codes, on surfaces that won't necessarily be viewed head-on.

The Me QR Code:

Somewhat more difficult. A three-step process. First, the background QR Code is created and saved and preserved. Next, in a duplicate file, the foreground QR Code color is deleted, creating a whitespace template stamp that can be used to cut white space out of my dark business suit. Next, my face is preserved to apply over the top of everything. Finally, the QR Code is assembled in layers. Original QR first (green), then my suit on top of it (now, blocking some of the white area), next the white background overlay pattern (to remove the white area again), then finally my smiling face (and hands) over the top (with a slightly enlarged head for a comical, bobble-head look). The effect is great, and the QR Code scans well. It's very helpful to use image processing software that allows independent layers for these processes (such as Adobe Photoshop), but not essential.

Food QR Code:

This was quite difficult. Each individual piece was hand selected for effect, rotated into position, sized and hand-placed. And the best part? Some scanning applications have trouble with it. Approximately five hours of work. Don't try this at home. I-Nigma performs well at scanning this code, but few others are able to do it reliably.

Figure 15 While extremely time-consuming, a hand-made QR Code can send a very powerful message.

Misc Tips & Tricks

There are a few basic concepts to keep in mind when doing this to your own QR Code. If you're not using a QR Code manager to archive your codes (such as what is done in the QRStuff.com system), you'll need to carefully archive your original QR Codes. Once you accidentally ruin one, you won't be able to re-generate it, because other generators won't encode it the same way, and sometimes even the same generators won't encode it the same way twice.

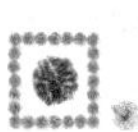
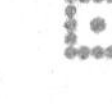

Skewing & Stretching: The QR Code below can be scanned just by tipping the book and scanning at a low angle. Stretching or compressing the image can be useful on oblique surfaces, or to make a QR Code suggestive of a less square object, such as the toolbox shown earlier in the chapter. Just pull it wider.

Outside the Box: Except for at the finder patterns, there's no reason to stay "inside the box." The "Quiet Zone" principle really only applies there. The dramatic effect of the "Me QR Code" above is due to the face and elbow leaving the square. Beyond drama, this is smart because any element *not* in the QR Code means less corrupted data *in* it. Do you have a long, horizontal or vertical object that you'd like in your code, such as a logo or company name? Try placing the left edge in the center of your QR Code, and allow it to protrude from the right side of the code. The effect is striking, and it scans nicely.

Way Outside the Box: Add extra context to the QR Codes, using entirely external art. There's no reason to modify your QR Code if you simply don't want to overcomplicate things. Add some art that is completely external to the QR Code, and add loads of interest and up the *cool* factor tremendously. Plus, once you've finished?

Frame Your QR Code: Create a custom frame for your QR Code that blends into the code and smoothes the edges. Include your C2A, recommended app download, etc. The tremendous benefit to this? A frame is re-usable, and can be applied around any QR Code you make in the future. Just paste in your QR Code, or lay it down over the top of the frame in a layout (you may need to trim down the Quiet Zone to do this. Use an abstract design like this one (I call it "Bubbles") or incorporate your own design elements. There's no limit to embellishments that can be made outside of the QR Code, since there's no risk of damaging it. Go for it! Note: The black circles around the corners of the QR Code do encroach on the quiet zone, so test well.

Multiple Copies: As the UnitagLive.com QR Codes demonstrate, there is no reason that a code must be a single color. It can, in fact, be many or even a whole fluid gradient of color. Try downloading multiple copies of a QR Code in differing colors, and then carefully cut & paste them together for placement at the transition between two other art elements for a more natural, organic effect, or perhaps an even more striking effect. Alternately, try slightly off-setting two colors for a high-contrast or 3-D look. Or download a very, very faintly colored QR Code (just barely perceptible from the white background), to use as a template to hand-draw a QR Code. See *Create a Template*, below.

Negative QR Codes: Unlike Datamatrix codes, QR Codes Will NOT scan if the white/dark space is reversed. However, that doesn't mean you can't smoothly blend a QR Code into a dark background. The complicated layers used in the *Me QR Code* are difficult to do, but what's very easy is to download a code and select and save the white space as a transparent image (white background color, transparent "alpha" background color) and use it to block out the background space, leaving other images showing through as the foreground. For best effect, crop out all of the Quiet Zone except for a narrow sliver.

Mirror QR Codes: While they won't scan if reversed (mirror image) either, that doesn't mean they can't be inverted on a transparent sticker, for viewing on the opposite side of a window, or on any transparent surface. Just select 'Flip Horizontal' in your image editor, or adjust the image settings in your layout software to reverse the image. *Can't scan? Come into our store to scan the correct side…*

Smoothing The Edges: Try rounding the corners or edges of a QR Code for a more natural, smooth-flowing feel, or simply to create visual interest with a *Swiss Cheese* effect. Increase the error correction to maximum, and then start nibbling away at the QR Code edges, in between the Finder Patterns (corner eyes). You'll be surprised at how much of the code can be nibbled away, while the QR Code still functions. This one began to fail right around this point.

Create a Template: Create and download your code in a very light, faint color, or entirely white, as done here, in shadow (from UnitagLive.com). Then, hand-embellish your QR Code using image-editing software, or simply print and color with markers, pencils or paints, then use a scanner to capture the final version. This is a strategy employed by Yiying Lu, the artist and designer responsible for the Twitter "Fail Whale," and she has a number of beautiful, hand-embellished, museum-quality works of QR Code art based on popular celebrities posted on her website at *www.yiyinglu.com.* You can also trace your QR Codes. Here's a tip: as suggested previously, with any art project, generate them extra large, and shrink after completing to hide errors and shaky hands.

Where to Put the Logo: Some areas of the QR Code are more sensitive than others. For best results, try to locate your artistic

Figure 16 Blocking QR Elements

embellishments in one of the areas noted in the above diagrams. The far left diagram is the least safe, since there are a number of vital features of the QR Code located in the left-most (9 o'clock) part of the matrix. Also, the first row of pixels bordering the eyes should not be obscured. Always use an image or logo with a transparent background, as these specified sizes won't work if *all* of the area is obscured. Rather, judiciously apply a logo, which is mostly empty *transparent* background space.

Disclaimer

Play with your QR Codes, get to know them and make them yours. But, it is easy to modify QR Codes beyond recognition and render them useless. Start small and work up to the more ambitious types of modification. Use an image editor that supports layers (preferably) or at a minimum, back up often with new filenames, so that you won't have to start again from zero after breaking a QR Code irreparably. Trial and error is the name of the game. Ruining a few is part of the learning process, but try to make it as painless as possible. Don't get too frustrated; this is supposed to be fun, right? The end result will be worth the effort

---

[1] *More than one Alignment Pattern is certainly possible. As the matrix size of the QR Code increases, more and more are added to help the scanner keep track of their locations. But, in keeping with the Best Practice of keeping the data content low, there really should never be more than one Alignment Pattern. Before you ever get to that point, you QR Code will already have become unreasonably dense.*

[2] *Yes, I wrote "decrease error correction". Here's why. Error correction is good when part of a QR Code may be damaged or obscured. But if the whole thing is blurry all over, error correction won't help. There still has to be mostly good data. High error correction adds complexity and density to the QR Code matrix, and if you find yourself in a situation where the QR Code might come out with suboptimal print quality, this is a bad thing. Lose the error correction (anything with a variable QR Code printed uniquely from a database is disposable, so you don't need it). Also, go for broke when it comes to shrinking the matrix size. Shorten the URL, or anything you can.*

[3] *If you attempt the 'logo upload' feature at Unitaglive.com, you will notice that the maximum logo size possible is puny. Far larger logos are possible, but must be done by hand. One trick I use for getting the most out of Unitag is to upload a file containing only white space instead of a logo. Then, Unitag's generator leaves a hole to at least clear out some of the central space for the logo, which will be added later.*

15. Enter URL Shortening

The concept of URL Shortening has been around since 2000, when U.S. Patent number 6957224 for a concept of "Efficient Retrieval of URLs," which describes in essence, precisely what a URL Shortener does: to use the words of the patent application language, it acts as a shorthand URL linking to a database, in which is stored the longhand URL, to which a visitor is redirected.

When Twitter Launched onto the scene, bringing with it a dream of instant publishing of concise, 142-character messages, it brought with it a new challenge for users: How to incorporate multiple @Mentions, #Hashtags, clickable URL links, and of course, offer text, a call-to-action, or a meaningful message, all in just 142-characters. This quickly became an exercise in efficiency, as well as an opportunity for new technologies to be developed. How to fit all this into the tiny space allotted (essentially the same as a basic Short Message Service (SMS) telephone text message.

Enter the URL Shortener

Twitter could never have become so popular and successful without URL shorteners. It's rarely useful to share just a single link to a website's main page. Preferrably, an more often than not, very specific content is linked, from deep within the file structure of a website, just as below. This *deep linking* means that URLs can be extraordinarily long. A URL shortener acts as an intermediate referrer, storing a reference to the long URL, and assigning it a shorter name. Then, when someone clicks on the link, in just a few milliseconds, the URL shortener looks up the short link in its database, and redirects the user's web browser to the original location that the long URL specifies.

Various online services will shorten URLs, by hosting a URL redirect on their site to a destination URL, and provide a smaller shorthand URL. For example, given the following long, *deep-linked* URL:

http://letsplay.offerpop.com/campaign/633178/entry/v34710?utm_campaign=Hebrew%20Academy%20Tampa&utm_source=Flyer2 (109 characters)

It's easy to see that 109 characters in *deep-linked* content such as this might have far too many characters to fit into a Tweet, SMS message, or any location where space and character count is at a premium. Using a URL shortener to your URL, and then provides a shorter link that sends a visitor to the same URL, such as the following:

http://bit.ly/helpha6 (21 characters)

Just as promised, the above URL, while small enough to fit nearly anywhere, sends visitors to the same location as the version five times longer.

The Importance of URL Shortening

Take, for example, the sample Twitter post (or "Tweet") at the beginning of this chapter. It consists of a mere 116 characters, due to the use of the bit.ly URL shortener. This makes it possible for the entire message to fit in the Tweet, whereas this would simply not be possible with the full URL.

Given the frequency with which files are automatically shared using Social Media feeds, etc, it is possible for a URL (including the protocol, URL, as well as subdomains, directories, filenames & even query strings) to exceed 142 characters on its own. So, shortening is vital. Take the following example:

http://www.yourwebsite.com/wp-content/posts/sales-articles/2013-03-12/name-of-your-article-here/?querystring=yourquery&querystring2=source[1]
(138 characters for URL alone)

Without URL Shortening, such a link, though typical these days, would be unusable. Clicking the shortened URL immediately redirects the visitor to the longer URL. So, when every character counts, URL shorteners have grabbed up many short domain names, especially for two-letter top level domains (the last part of the URL, ie, ".ly"), since that shaves off an additional letter, as well as opening up another source of URLs, since it is exceedingly difficult to find a good .com or .org URL; there aren't many good ones left.

So, for this reason, shortening URLs has become an essential social media strategy, because it is simply neater, prettier, and easier to type than the long URL, which is impossible to type accurately, especially if it contains automatically-generated tokens, etc… even if someone was motivated to attempt it. Reasons for shortening:

- *It makes the URL simply shorter, so that it can fit into a Tweet, SMS text message, or above the "break line[2]" in a Facebook, Wordpress, CMS or other Social Media post.*
- *It makes the URL shorter, so that it will not break across lines in an email, web page, or document, and be rendered un-clickable. This happens frequently in Email clients or word processors that automatically insert line breaks at 84-character intervals, or potentially any time that a URL is longer than the page it needs to be displayed on. This also happens when emails are forwarded, and hard line breaks and indents are added for the included message, as well as in plain-text emails, where long-tailed, deep-linked, or query-string URLs aren't hidden behind a link, but are visible in the email body.*
- *It makes the URL neater and possible for a person to type, if necessary (especially if used with a human-readable keyword).*
- *It generally provides click-through statistics, and enables non-techies to track their responses*

Some URL Shortening services:

- *Ow.ly – The shortener of Social Media service Hoot Suite*
- *Goo.gl – Google's public shortener*
- *t.co – Perhaps the shortest shortener out there, t.co is operated by Twitter for their service.*
- *Tr.im – Another popular choice*
- *Qrs.ly – QrStuff.com's shortener.*
- *Eshlepper.com/shorten – My own short URL, reserved specifically for shortening & QR Code applications for clients; an example of a very short URL that can be obtained. It is also an example of the easy-to-configure YOURLS system, detailed in later chapters, for 'vanity' URL Shortening, on any domain you choose.*
- *Bit.ly – Public & Free URL shortening service – even allows customization of the shortcode link, as seen above: Bit.ly/helpha6 is a custom "Bit Link," for ease of reading, typing, and branding. Bit.ly can also be used remotely via API, and can be integrated with your own custom domain name (turning your own website into a "whatever.ly"' URL shortener equal in capabilities to bit.ly.*

How Is This Important for QR Codes?

Once you begin to create QR Codes, you will want to direct the visitor to specific locations on the internet, most likely your website. In order to do so, you're going to eventually want to encode more information in the QR Code than can be gracefully encoded: for example, one of these long-tailed, deep-linked, or query-string appended URL.

As we discussed in earl chapters, a QR Code can store data that is practically unlimited, up to more than 7,000 characters. However, as the quantity of data stored increases, the QR Code becomes more and more complicated, eventually exceeding the ability of a camera & Smart Phone to read them properly, even under the best conditions. I see them all the time: overly complicated QR Codes that are impossible to scan, or nearly so. Take the following example QR Codes, one encoded with only the short version of a URL, and one encoded with a full version without using a shortener, that you'll never be able to scan in million bazillion years (for a very large version that is hopefully scannable… see the end of the chapter):

Figure 17 Shortened vs. Unshortened URL in QR Code

This QR Code is a shortened version of the one below, which is packed with an entire paragraph of data. Depending on the medium in which you're reading this book, it may or may not be possible to scan it at all... at almost any size, and certainly not the reasonably sized version shown below. This makes such a QR Code useless for nearly any purpose, and yet, this doesn't even begin to push the limits of how much data can be stored. The table below gives an idea of how the length of a URL stored in a QR Code affects the size of the matrix, and the complexity of the code.

This is an extreme example of simply storing too much data in the QR Code. But it's not necessary. The same data can be stored by using a URL shortener, with the bulk of the data sent to the user's Smart Phone browser upon scanning, and only a shortened link to the information's location actually stored in the QR Code. The shortened version of the QR Code directs the user to the same data, but only actually encodes the location of the data. This makes for a graceful, easy-to-scan QR Code for any purpose. See the end of this chapter for an enlarged version.

Tweets have an absolute fixed length, and anything beyond 142 characters is simply cut off. However, with QR Codes, as the data stored increases, the code becomes more and more densely coded, slowly becoming more difficult to decipher. This is what's known as "degrading gracefully": it gradually becomes more and more difficult to read, and ultimately impossible. Because a QR Code degrades gracefully, it's difficult to say precisely how much data is too much to try to encode, since this can be subjective, depending on many factors:

- *Planned size of the QR Code in print.*
- *Expected distance of the scanner from the QR Code.*
- *Level of error correction needed.*
- *Expected condition of QR Code & possible damage or wear.*
- *Lighting and QR Code contrast*
- *Data density*
- *Characteristics of the encoder.*

However, there are fixed points as which the size of the QR Code matrix increases. This means that within certain limits, additional data doesn't necessarily result in a higher-resolution QR Code.

Note again the diagram below, re-printed from the previous chapter, which lays out the approximate points at which the increases in barcode density take place. Note that in the top row, for the simplest possible full-size QR Code, there is the potential for 25, 20, 16, or 10 alphanumeric characters to be encoded while keeping the simplest QR Code matrix size of 21x21 pixels (modules)[3]. Thus, a QR Code with low error correction (L) suitable for printing in a place where it is most likely to remain intact and legible, can store around 25 alphanumeric characters without needing to increase the matrix size, resolution, and data coding density.

Sample Matrix Sizes vs. URL Length (and Error Correction)					
Version	Code Size WidthxHeight:	Low EC:	Medium EC:	Quality EC:	High EC:
1	21x21 Squares	25	20	16	10
2	25x25 Squares	47	38	29	20
3	29x29 Squares	77	61	47	35
4	33x33 Squares	114	90	67	50
5	37x37 Squares	154	122	87	64
6	41x41 Squares	195	154	108	84
7	45x45 Squares	224	178	125	93
8	49x49 Squares	279	221	157	122
9	53x53 Squares	335	262	189	143
10	57x57 Squares	395	311	221	174

Sample QR Code Matrix Sizes (color indicates safe, suspect & excessive data density)

For example: "http://www.YourSite.com" has 23 characters. Longer than that, as is usually the case, and your generator will end up in the 25x25 matrix level to incorporate all the characters you need. So, unless you are fortunate enough to be a Fortune 500 Company with a single-word URL name, or crafty enough to have a short business name URL, or instead opt to shorten the URL, this will create difficulty. As stated, the ideal is to encode your entire URL directly into the QR Code matrix, so that it will link directly to the destination site, without the need for intermediate referrers. But, of course, this can be technically demanding to execute without some web development expertise.

So, few businesses have such short URLs as to allow use of the 21x21 matrix (without using a URL shortener). But most should be able to use the 25x25 matrix without difficulty, even if directing to a specific web page on a site, with up to 47 characters in length (line 2 of the table below).

Is Direct Access, or Shortening Better?

The answer is YES. True, I did say that both ways are the best way. As in most aspects of life, there are trade-offs to be made, based on conflicting priorities. There are clear and undeniable benefits to both strategies, and each individual needs to assess which is best for their needs.

First, when linking directly to your content (which is presumably on your site), a friendly URL, *your own URL* is used. The visitor recognizes your company's URL, name and identity. This builds confidence and brand identity, as well as presenting a safe, secure and well-crafted image for your visitors. It keeps your web presence consistent, of a uniform look and feel, as well as reinforcing your company's website name. It's always the "*best*" way, and will usually be the way that professional, Managed Solutions are done (alternately, a subdomain of the agency's website is common).

Also, for many users, like small business owners with limited technical abilities in web design & implementation, there are a number of aspects of the direct URL Access strategy that will likely exceed their technical abilities; there are a number of hurdles to overcome, and these are just a few.

- *Using CMS pages as Landing Pages, for example, may leave you with URLs that are simply too long to gracefully store in a QR Code.*
- *Implementing Google Analytics code (or another traffic tracking scheme) to track your page visits may be beyond the ability of novices, and requires at least a small amount of doing, usually a bit of HTML hand-editing skill. Often it is easier just to shorten the URL; the quantity and quality of information won't be the same, but if you're working with a budget (in terms of money, time, and expertise), it will have to do.*
- *Appending query strings and other data to identify the specific source of traffic may also drive up the quantity of data needed, and require shortening.*
- *You'd better get it perfect, because coding directly into the QR Code matrix leaves no room for error. If a Landing Page is coded into the QR Code wrong, or accidentally deleted or changed after the fact, it's impossible to re-direct.*
- *If you've invested time and money in creating a Designer QR Code, using a dynamic (editable) shortener will stretch your budget by recycling it, making it possible to re-code your fancy, expensive QR Code on the back end and re-use it indefinitely. In such a case, the shortener is encoded in the QR Code matrix, and the destination URL is edited in the shortener system to change the destination URL.*
- *Subdomain setup and management, the key alternative, can be technically difficult.*

So, for all of these potent reasons, there are certainly advantages for the *average* user to shorten every URL used in a QR Code.

Planning To Fail & Leaving Room For Error

I've seen so many QR Codes that don't work, because their Landing Pages have been moved out from under them, like a rug in a slapstick comedy routine. Most QR Codes I see in the wild do not work. Obviously, perfection is the ideal, but much can go wrong. I acknowledge my own fallibility. I've made costly, stupid mistakes, and I relish the idea of always having a quick fix handy to prevent disaster when I make my next one, which I'm statistically overdue for, since I've really been spot on lately… knock on wood. So, consider URL shortening as a compromise; less perfect, but safer.

URL Shortening as a Best Practice

Thus, as one of my primary recommended Best Practices (and discussed simultaneously with Direct URL Access as a conflicting Best Practice), my advice is to always keep URLs as short as possible [as the primary best practice, or (if that's not practical for the use case[4]) use a URL shortener to keep QR Code matrices at the lowest possible resolution. Whether this means using a public URL shortener, or self-hosting your own shortener or mobile site (see later chapters on both of these options), depends on your personal preferences and technical ability. This will make for a neat, consistent look to QR Codes, and enable many of the other features discussed in this book to work, including creating Designer QR Codes. When using a shortened URL encoded in a QR Code, there are many benefits:

- *Metrics and click-through reports from the shortening service.*
- *Allows collection of metrics, even when the content is hosted on someone else's site, and other methods of analytics are impossible.*[5]
- *Uniform appearance of QR Codes (recognizable to consumer)*
- *Fastest scanning for the user (due to simplicity)*
- *Accurate recognition by all QR Code readers (due to simplicity)*
- *Smaller printed size is possible, when space is a concern (always)*
- *Reliable duplication, even through photocopying, offset printing, silk-screening on fabric, rubber stamping, or other printing methods that don't allow for the precise rendering or resolution possible with digital printing.*
- *Reliable use online if needed, as the simple size allows for larger QR Code display less susceptible to screen dithering distortion (an issue on many computer monitors or televisions, as well as QR Code scanning apps)*
- *Redirection/reassignment & editing of the URL after production or printing, to change the message offer text, making the QR Code durable and re-usable or, in the worst-case, to direct it to the correct location if a coding error is discovered after printing.*
- *Lower resolution presents more after-processing artistic additions*
- *To permit secure, password-protected access to the site content, if needed. Obviously, for marketing purposes, usually the broadest possible access is desired, but there are certainly times to limit access… all of which are beyond the scope of this book, but some shorteners will stop visitors and ask for a password, if you choose, notably: QRStuff.com's shortener.*

- *Subjective 'better,' more distinctly QR-y appearance.*

Exceptions to 'Shorten Everything'

But of course, every rule has its exception, and this rule has a single important exception, as well, which is: *When the information must be available off-line.*

The vast majority of the time, you'll be directing traffic to your website (or a mobile-optimized Landing Page containing...), social media accounts, YouTube videos, vCard information, or any number of things that are available only online, using your Smart Phone's internet browser or any number of on-board applications that access the internet and display the media.

Sometimes, and this will be very rare, you may want a specific message available upon QR Code scan that is available directly, without the necessity of an internet connection. This may be in locations that lack wireless service, or in warehouses constructed so as to block cellular signals. Since the QR Code is able to actually store the information in the code itself, the QR Code reader will be able to display the message, even without an Internet connection. Sample applications can include:

- *When MeCard/vCard info is coded directly into QR Code matrix*[6]
- *Locations without cellular service*
- *Locations that block radio signals (either by design or by accident)*
- *Areas with high radio interference (industrial)*
- *Messages that shouldn't be readable by the casual observer*
- *Safety-related messages that need to be available at all times*
- *When there is a need to read the data directly, without using a web browser to resolve the shortened data, such as fax servers*

For these situations, and some may be difficult to imagine, all the data can be store in the QR Code matrix; This can be enough to write an entire chapter of a book in a QR Code. Actually, that sounds like a really interesting idea. Let's try that!

The giant QR Code here on the next page encodes the following information:

Time and time again, I try to ram home the importance of QR Code "Best Practices." Nothing is as important as ensuring that the QR Codes you generate are indeed scannable. And, the most basic factor that bears on whether a user can scan your QR Code is the quantity of data you choose to encode. By the time you've added hundreds of characters of text or URL-Appended data, your QR Code has become all but unreadable. This is the classic example of too much information. Don't forget that "Q.R." stands for "Quick Response." Standing around waiting for the perfect light to scan a 1000-Byte extravaganza is just stupid. Don't do this. Shorten your QR. Please. Help me help you. I could have done worse, but you get the idea, right? No?

Best Practices!

Keep it short!

Shorten it!

Don't Get Greedy!

We'd all love our contact information to Magically pop up and store on a user's smart phone. But, it's just too much data. If the technology doesn't allow for this efficiency, shorten it! Quick & easy.

---

[1] *Some of these links have been edited as examples, with descripting keywords inserted to illustrate the different parts of the URL. As such, they don't necessarily have a destination, and may not work.*

[2] *Most content is displayed on websites in full, but also frequently as a short introduction, extract or blurb. The exact size depends on the system, but usually, only the first 50 words or so is visible, and presented with a clickable link for 'Read More..." or some such. That point is known as the*

break line, and it is vitally important to get content "Above the break line" so that it will be visible immediately to site visitors, who may never click on it and reach the content otherwise.

[3] *No two QR Code generators are equal, which is why you could create QR Codes from multiple generators with the same content that look dramatically different. Any discussion of the exact number of characters that determines when a QR Code generator increases the matrix size (or "Version) and adds modules to accommodate the additional data is always imprecise. It is entirely dependent on the exact coding that results from a given generator algorithm, the error correction level, etc. These numbers are provided for demonstration purposes.*

[4] *The reason why keeping the URL short is impractical for the use case is irrelevant. In most cases, it's simply that the technology needed to preserve other best practices isn't available at the budget (of time, energy, manpower, bandwidth and money) required. That's perfectly acceptable. Whether the budget is $10, $100 or $100 Million – the budget is the budget, and that's that. The launch date is the launch date, and further fiddling is impossible. No shame in this game.*

[5] *This is yet another key reason that URL shorteners are so often used on social media sites; length isn't always the key issue. While, for content on one's own website, there's sure to be mountains of analytics information available on site visitors, this is owing to code embedded in the site, and not available to others. When sharing on Facebook, Twitter, LinkedIn, etc,* ***you*** *are that other, who gets no data. However, by sharing with a short link, visitors make a quick stop (imperceptible milliseconds) on a system you control to be counted for a moment, and then forwarded on to the destination.*

[6] *iOS, for example, does not allow direct file downloads from the internet of vCards. Rather, iPhone users must either have vCards emailed to them, or scan it directly from vCard-formatted into the QR Code matrix.*

16. Advanced Strategies

In addition to the techniques discussed in earlier chapters, there are a number of techniques that are generally beyond the ability or need of casual QR Code users and most small businesses. These techniques will be of interest and use almost exclusively for professionals, due to the level of complexity involved, technical overhead (including website hosting, data processing, variable data printing (VDP), processing bandwidth & memory for image rendering, as well as other factors). It would be a rare small business owner who would personally use the information in this chapter for their own needs. Rather, this is the domain of experts who need to produce QR Codes on a massive scale, usually 30,000-100,000 codes in a single batch, or even up to several million.

These users include:

- *Marketing Professionals*
- *Direct Mail Producers*
- *Mailing Services*
- *Commercial Printers*
- *Magazine Publishers*
- *Business Development Centers*
- *Response-Tracking Professionals*
- *Search Engine Marketing (SEM) Pros*
- *Search Engine Optimization (SEO) Pros*
- *Website & Social Media Developers*
- *Web Analytics Professionals*
- *Researchers*

"Dynamic" QR Codes can be confusing, as this term is applied to a few things:

First, there are QR Codes that are redirected after scanning (ie, the actual destination is not encoded in the data, but rather just the referrer/shortener). These have the advantage of being re-configurable AFTER print production or deployment – perhaps to save a campaign from the jaws of death.

Second, QR Codes that are fixed, but mass produced with variable content (perhaps a unique code for each direct mail recipient written with variable data) to allow tracking by individual recipient.

Either is commonly referred to as "Dynamic" – but the latter is probably better labelled "variable content."

Dynamic QR Codes:

Changeable Landing Pages make a QR Code re-usable. The effort and expense of crafting a designer QR Code is wasted when the offer expires, URL changes, or is no longer needed. Making the URL changeable without affecting the QR Code image is essential to get the best longevity and economy out of any QR Codes, whether a given code is a simple black & white code (and would only need a few minutes to replace), or a multi-color designer extravaganza that was created at great expense of time and money, in cooperation with a professional design or advertising firm. This is a main reason that shortening URLs is recommended.

On-The-Fly QR Code Generation: For the typical deployment of a QR Code, one needs merely to visit a generator site and create a QR Code image in a few seconds. However, what if, hypothetically, you need to generate a QR Code for a URL that you don't know yet. Like, for example, if you want QR Code to be generated for every page of your Blog, automatically for the visitors. An excellent option for this would be to insert a QR Code formatted using variable text (such as a mail or data merge) to make a call to the Google Charts API (as mentioned previously), automatically generating a QR Code for any data or URL.

Obviously, experienced Web Programmers will be able to take advantage of this quite readily, but even novices should be able to easily add some on-the-fly QR Code generation capabilities to their work.

Sending Data with a QR Code:

Most of the focus for applications is getting the user information from the site. Now, the usual way that things work is that a URL is coded into the QR Code, and the web page is fetched. For this purpose, as stated repeatedly, it is advisable for many reasons to keep the data short and sweet, to keep the data stored in the QR Code at an absolute minimum.

However, there is a reason to do the precise opposite; to encode as much data in the QR Code as possible. Generally, the QR Code doesn't encode any information about the person scanning it. Instead, it simply decodes the URL and passes the URL to the Smart Phone's browser. However, we can flip this concept around. Just as the website sends loads of information to the mobile user's web browser, we can encode massive quantities of information in the QR Code, for the user's web browser to upload. What information will the QR Code send about the user?

Well, anything we decide. Here's how it works: Any valid URL encoded in the QR Code will be passed on to the browser and sent to the website. What few laymen understand completely is that data can be added, or appended, to the end of a URL. You've probably glanced up into your browser window at some point and noticed that the URL is extremely long and complicated, with various random strings of numbers. These numbers are not random. They identify you to the website, and are passed along from page to page as you navigate, keeping track of your status, progress, shopping cart, cookies, or any number of things. You can do this, as well. This is called a ***Query String*** or ***URL-Appended Data***, and it works like this:

```
http://www.Website.com/?keyword1=yes&keyword2
=no¹
```

Adding your own keywords to the URL that you encode in your QR Code is as simple as that. What this will do, is send two values to the web server. These values can be manipulated in many ways. They can be used to pre-fill fields of a web form. They can also be accessed directly using a web script. For example, add the following to your site's HTML, and the keyword value will be automatically plucked from the URL and used on your page; the following web page, when requested using the above URL outputs the following:

Keyword#1 is yes!

Keyword #2 is no!

```
<html>
  <head></head>
  <body>
      <p>Keyword #1 is <?php echo
$_GET['keyword1']; ?>!</p>
      <p>Keyword #2 is <?php echo
$_GET['keyword2']; ?>!</p>
  </body>
</html>
```

This can be a great way to greet your visitors by name, etc. It's a great strategy used to accompany using unique QR Codes for each recipient; alternately, you can use this method to pre-populate a web form to make form completions easier, or populate a hidden form field that tells the visitor's source, or from whence they were referred.

Query Strings can also be used to track clicks of the URL via Google Analytics, which has its own keywords that can be used to track campaigns. The GA script on your web page will capture and recognize the GA campaign keywords appended to your link (or QR Code-encoded link) and track traffic, along with other Google Analytics data.

Completely Unique QR Codes:

Over the course of hundreds of direct mail campaigns that I've personally crafted, overseen, tracked, and studied, I've become a believer in the importance of detailed response tracking. Ultimately, no one running a marketing program, whether for business or not, wants to be bogged down in the nitty-gritty of response tracking; they just want their marketing efforts to magically work, bring in customers, generate sales, and make money. Rinse, repeat. That's understandable. But, that also assumes that everything works perfectly, as well as possible, every single time, and there is no way to improve. But, what happens, in that *extremely unlikely scenario* where a marketing campaign underperforms and doesn't have the intended success? Or doesn't have the maximum success possible? Or simply falls flat, leaving no evidence that it ever took place… just a waste of money?

Direct mail, in particular presents a great many challenges for marketers. First and foremost, the high cost of entry can be prohibitive, as even low-cost mailers can cost between $0.50-0.75 each. $0.25 per piece on postage alone is a given. Add to that printing costs, artwork, additional services for tracking the response, time and energy.

Graphic design and layout can be difficult to find on a budget, or very time consuming to do on ones own. Further, the deepest discounts come at high volumes (10,000 pieces or more) and working with commercial printers. For the Do-It-Yourself-er, direct mail can quickly turn into a full-time job for the business owner, and potentially bankrupt a small business: if done wrong, it's just money spent. All the return-on-investment statistics in the world don't mean a hill of beans when blunders are made.

The Upside to Direct Mail?

It's the third most effective method of advertising, right behind knocking on a customer's door, or calling them on the phone. But it certainly must be done right. Gauging response and interest in a promotion can be daunting, however. Often, there isn't a very effective way of determining which customers respond best to an offer, where they are, and how they found you. For powerful businesses at the top of their industry, this is preaching to the choir, as they already know this, and actively implement programs to counter this and track response.

QR Codes give the professional marketer the ability to put a unique QR Code onto every single mail piece sent out in a campaign. Thus, when a customer scans the QR Code, not only are they viewing your marketing message, but they are also disclosing to the sender which QR Code was scanned, and thus, indirectly (or directly) their name & address, list segment, approximate location, latitude and longitude, if their mobile device allows it, and potentially even appended Google Analytics meta data tags to assist in collecting visitor information from your site.[2]

Accomplishing the pre-formatting is a significant technical feat, which I've coded a number of tools to ease, available on the website. But once the data processing is done, commercial mailers should be able to get this done with little effort, and will have access to services such as the United States Postal Service's PostalOne system, RIBBS, and other tools that leverage the Postal Service's IMB (Intelligent Mail Barcode) system to tell the disposition of every single piece of mail in a mailing, in realtime.

iAccutrace (iaccutrace.com)

iAccutrace is a commercial service built primarily on the United States Postal Service's Intelligent Mail Barcode system, and offered through a number of commercial printing and mailing services. iAccutrace provides comprehensive tracking at the individual-piece level. While the primary thrust of iAccutrace is monitoring in-home delivery performance for these direct mailings: recording automated scans of the discrete IMB barcodes on mailers while in the USPS delivery system, the concept itself lends itself to a number of ancillary functions, and integrates QR Code functionality within the system, recording QR Code scans (ie, web page visits and redirects), and acts as a URL shortener, referring traffic to the appropriate campaign landing page.

So, if pure metrics on click-throughs are all that's desired, this can be a great, no-nonsense way to integrate uniquely-coded QR Codes into a direct mail campaign, particularly where one's own landing pages and/or technical abilities aren't up to the task of tracking this on the landing page itself.

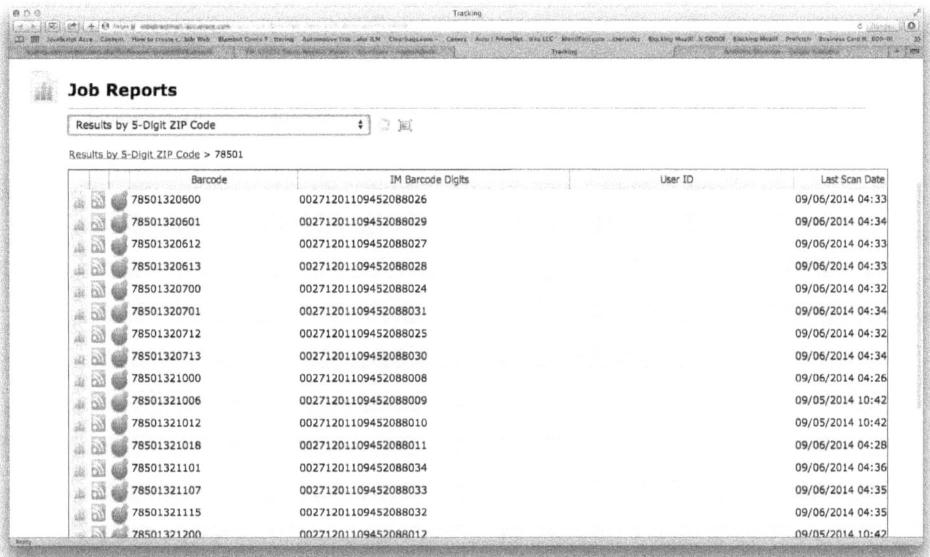

Tracking

Job Reports

Results by 5-Digit ZIP Code

Results by 5-Digit ZIP Code > 78501

Barcode	IM Barcode Digits	User ID	Last Scan Date
78501320600	00271201109452088026		09/06/2014 04:33
78501320601	00271201109452088029		09/06/2014 04:34
78501320612	00271201109452088027		09/06/2014 04:33
78501320613	00271201109452088028		09/06/2014 04:33
78501320700	00271201109452088024		09/06/2014 04:32
78501320701	00271201109452088031		09/06/2014 04:34
78501320712	00271201109452088025		09/06/2014 04:32
78501320713	00271201109452088030		09/06/2014 04:34
78501321000	00271201109452088008		09/06/2014 04:26
78501321006	00271201109452088009		09/05/2014 10:42
78501321012	00271201109452088010		09/05/2014 10:42
78501321018	00271201109452088011		09/06/2014 04:28
78501321101	00271201109452088034		09/06/2014 04:36
78501321107	00271201109452088033		09/06/2014 04:35
78501321115	00271201109452088032		09/06/2014 04:35
78501321200	00271201109452088012		09/05/2014 10:42

RIBBS is, of course, a public service. Mailers and end-users of any size can sign up for a business account at http://ribbs.usps.com to set up mailer ids and learn about the system. Signup really only entails filling out a form, downloading the fonts, and printing some test data to prove you can do it competently and not snarl the whole system with faulty barcodes.

Alternately, working with a professional mail fulfillment service (call me) can get this done without the effort of all this troubleshooting, testing, account setup and enrollments.

EasyPurl (easypurl.com)

EasyPURL also makes its business on what is called "1:1" (one-to-one) marketing. The concept of 1:1 marketing is that, as opposed to thy typical mass-marketing ads you might see on television, in which everyone sees the same ad, the 1:1 marketing paradigm means that each visitor is shown a unique, customized marketing message. Of course, knowing who these visitors are, in advance, is essential. For a typical non-mass marketing campaign, ie, other than television, magazine, radio, outdoor billboards: those visitors generated by email, direct mail, etc, 1:1 marketing provides the opportunity to deliver a better, more targeted ad to your prospects, personalized by an endless array of factors: your prospect's name, the vehicle they own, the language they speak, purchase history, or even gender, etc.

PURLs: personalized URLs are a de facto standard way of sending along identifying information to your website with each response. Essentially, a PURL is precisely what we're discussing here: a unique URL that is dedicated and unique to a single responding consumer, although in this case, it may or may not be encoded into a QR Code. An example of a PURL might be any of the following:

www.Daniel.Benjamin.Auto-Values.com

www.DanielBenjamin1234.Auto-Values.com

The key difference between a PURL and QR Codes is of course that the QR Code need not be human-readable; An eye toward efficiency, using all available character and number combinations will yield a gain in terms of character count, which means lower data load, simpler QR Code matrix (perhaps a one or two version level gain), increased security (as you are not sending any user information over the internet, not even a first name), etc.

http://Auto-Values.com/1fR682

For Professional Use

For a professional printer, I only provide short codes, and they will be able to insert the QR Codes by generating them as they print, using dedicated software. When doing this, certainly be careful to keep a lid on the length of the URLs. Just because they can be encoded, doesn't mean they should be encoded. The same rules apply. Don't expect your printer to fully comprehend what it entails to get the job done right: that's your job, using the information in this book.

Figure 18 By decoding, it's revealed that these codes are subtly different and send different data to the web server.

Most can print the QR Codes just fine, but certainly won't shorten them for you to make sure they scan properly. Note that QR Codes have no absolute need to be human-readable, to whereas a Also, bear in mind that printing errors happen, and fuzziness or blurriness is possible, particularly on glossy papers, and particularly for inkjet printers. So, keep it simple and the data load low for fault tolerance.

For the DIY Job:

For a do-it-yourself-er planning to mail their own campaign, the simplest method is to download (purchase may be required, many are available online) a QR Code printing plugin or barcode plugin that supports QR Code printing for Microsoft Word, or another program that facilitates it. Assign the proper column in your data file to a field using the Mail Merge function, and print away.

It's also possible to actually export the QR Code images and insert them into the MS Word document via filename using a Data or Mail Merge. A description of this process can be found in an article on my web site, as well as in the site blog at WebMerge.me, an excellent service that I recommend that can help in automating processes like this for the beginner. Configure a PDF form, or Microsoft Word document, or build a merge file online, then upload a list and merge away. The files can be sent to email addresses within the list, one address, etc. Further, Jeremy Clarke, my contact at WebMerge was very helpful in the past, assisting with rabidly making available new features to suit our needs.

Alternately, companies that produce label printers, notably Brother, Inc (brother.com) publish software for use with their label printers that has great capabilities. Before purchasing a pricey QR Code plugin, consider spending $30-$60 on a Brother P-Touch label printer. Each comes complete with Brother's P-Touch Editor software, which makes building mail-merge documents a breeze, in every label size they support, or simply create an 8.5x11" document and merge a QR Code into your letter. As of this writing, the P-Touch Editor software could be downloaded for free from the Brother website, independent of a printer purchase, which can easily handle lightweight document creation (don't expect Microsoft Word feature levels) with integrated barcode printing. I happen to own the Brother P-Touch U-570, which is excellent for quickly merging a QR Code onto a mailing label. Equipped with their continuous (non-perforated) labels, it can churn out labels of any size, on demand, and slice them off ready to stick.

Pre-Populating Web Forms

As a demonstration of this concept, it's possible to generate entirely unique QR Codes for every recipient of a mail campaign, so that each scan reveals the identity of the recipient. Ultimately, the QR Code is simply a printed symbol, just as readable as name and address information that is being printed on a mail piece. Try these two QR Codes, for example; one a blank web form landing page, and one, the same web form pre-coded and pre-populated with test data for a simulated direct mail recipient. This data was sent using URL-appended Query Strings corresponding to the form fields, and accessing Formstack.com's API commands.

Mobile visitors will arrive with the majority of their data pre-filled in the form (this is a Formstack.com form). Although in this example, the data is immediately visible on the form itself (and changeable), it could just as easily be hidden and read-only, and the visitor would simply be asked for far less information, an equally attractive proposition that boosts response.

The specifics of how to do this is the realm of computer processing, and is beyond the pale of what an average, casual user would like to do on their own. But my own preferred method is to use Microsoft Excel spreadsheets to format the data together into a single text string which complies with the API (Application Programming Interface) of either the Wufoo or Formstack form hosting service (the latter has some advantages, in my view).

Once the Query-String-appended URLs are generated in the Excel Spreadsheet, they will be far longer than can be coded gracefully into a QR Code. So, they must be shortened. There are a number of ways to do this. I've had excellent results formatting the short URLs and shortening them with the QRStuff.com shortener, which has an excellent bulk upload capability, and also with shortening URLs using YOURLS. The former was used for most of my professional applications, but YOURLS was used for this example.

SECURITY ALERT!

Just because you can send data to the form doesn't mean you should. Bear in mind that you shouldn't be sending your customer or lead's private information helter-skelter across the Internet. All web traffic is subject to intercept and exploitation.

These are just examples to illustrate the concept dramatically. In real life, names, addresses, contact information, etc, should be handled by scripts on the web server side, and not exposed by sending from client to server:

1. ***Where data is appended to a URL as in the "query string" examples or "dynamic URL" examples above, the ideal is for this data to be non-personally-identifiable – ie, not name, address, etc, and certainly not phone, email, SSN, etc.***
2. ***While passing personal information is certainly convenient for accessing it on the server side, adding it to the query string is extremely insecure, and legally problematic in more and more locales. Using anonymous identifiers to match to PII information in a server-side database is the more secure option that should be used in all cases.***

Automatically Collating Forms

Similarly, Adobe Acrobat (Professional Version) has excellent QR Code generation abilities. From any form created using Adobe Acrobat, a barcode field can be selected, just like any text or numerical field. In just a few clicks, a savvy user can create a web-linked form that can be filled in and printed by an end-user, and the data can be automatically read via QR Code scan, sent via Webhook to a database, or to an online Form for collection and storage.

Vanity Friendly Shortening

An ingenious and elegant way to host your own , the best way is to use Your Own URL Shortener (YOURLS) to set up your own URL shortener on a web server. Then, you can easily upload your list of extremely long & complex URLs and shorten them, in bulk. To do this, you'll need to install the YOURLS System, which is automatic for GoDaddy hosted sites -- just find the 'Applications' section of your hosting manager and install it in a few clicks, and otherwise still very simple if you are able to use an FTP client. After setting up YOURLS, download and install the following useful plugins.

- *QR Code generation plugin (or)*
- *Inline QR Code plugin*
- *Query String Forward*
- *Allow Hyphens (in short keywords)*
- *Bulk Upload plugin – enables upload of a .CSV (Comma-Separated Values) list of short codes and long codes to store. This will be required for a large-scale campaign with unique, trackable QR Codes.*

This can also be done using QR Stuff's (www.QRStuff.com) shortener, but using your own shortener has several very potent advantages. You control the short code, and can decide when you upload it, precisely what it will be for each QR Code on your list. For example, you could shorten your code to:

`MyContestSite.com/JohnDoe3`

This will make your code very friendly and inviting, as well as interesting to the recipient, and make them very curious to visit it. Additionally, this allows for the creation of a short code that can be easily typed by the recipient, even if they don't make it their business to scan QR Codes.

---

[1] *The terms "keyword1" and "keyword2" are completely arbitrary, as are the values assigned to each, after the equals sign (=). You can call them whatever you like. Give them descriptive names to designate which QR Code was scanned. For example, if multiple QR Codes were generated for placement in different locations, advertisements, or publications, the query strings would be passed to the website, and recorded by your analytics software (or alternately, your webform). Thus, this value can be used to secretly "tattle" on your scanning customers.*

[2] *Google Analytics allows the creation of named campaigns and codes, which are used to tag links in precisely the above fashion, using proprietary keywords. When a site visitor lands on your web page, the Google Analytics code records these keywords and values, which feed into the GA dashboard for recording their response, along with other data tracked in GA.*

[3] *Of course, bear in mind that a shortener keyword must be unique. Multiple John Does on a list would create problems; for this reason, adding a unique identifier to the list (or alternately, numbering the John Does) is essential to maintaining uniqueness, and is a chief feature of any PURL implementation.*

17. Case Studies

In the pages that follow, I detail several concepts in QR Code marketing that I've employed to leverage QR Codes in some very interesting and unique ways.

Several of these amount to simple examples of mailers and QR Codes. But admittedly, some reach far beyond that, and their execution involves some advanced web development skill, database programming, landing page design, browser detection, cookie-setting, and a host of other concepts that raise the technical bar very high.

Potential clients who would like more information on managed implementations like these are encouraged to contact the author for more information or consultation.

It is not expected that this should serve as complete instructions for all aspects of these processes such that these techniques could be easily duplicated with the descriptions herein. Rather, these advanced ideas are provided as general brainstorming and ideating.

Showtime QR Code

On the facing page is an example of a QR Code concept that my company created for a client. As mentioned earlier in the book, I discussed the idea of a QR Code that was simply *not for the use of the consumer*. Rather, it's more of a point-of-sale barcode that allows the business to scan coupons and offers brought in by their mail recipients to gauge the impact of their marketing efforts, which is why it is very much on the small side, lacks a call to action, etc.

This particular client was very savvy to wanting to gauge the merits and effectiveness of their direct mail marketing, and had a history of offering employees a cash "bounty" (AKA a "spiff") for mailers they could collect from visiting customers, specifically to have a record of this. Most businesses do something of the sort, collecting and counting mailers, correlating them with product purchases, etc. It's an essential part of marketing: evaluating the marketing effort's success (or lack thereof).

But collecting stacks of mailers and hand-counting them is not an ideal solution: They get lost. They are mis-counted. Even the best of intentions in this scenario means extreme amounts of work and potential errors and inaccuracies, especially if individual mailers are correlated with actual sales. We initially conceived of a very small QR Code that wasn't intended for customers to scan at all: it was exclusively for the client's record-keeping. But of course, the obvious question is "What if the consumer scans it… what happens then?"

Admittedly, this is a bizarre reversal. The solution is something we dubbed "Showtime". It combines an intelligent mobile landing page system that directs consumers to a dedicated campaign landing page that promotes the offer further, as well as accomplishing an instant contact capture that identifies the consumer (the uniquely coded QR Code is matched in a back-end database to their original contact information from the mailing… and in this case, information on their recent purchases, type of vehicle they drive, current values, etc).

But the real magic of "Showtime" is on the landing page: When a authorized (cookie carried in the device's browser) device scans it (ie, the client's staff), it directs them to a mobile dashboard that allows them to access the above contact information, vehicle information, and other data about the consumer, as well as update the record with the disposition of the customer's visit: A sold vehicle and $30,000 revenue? A service visit of $600? All recorded, collated and archived for future analysis

Static Campaign QR Code

While not an advanced QR Code implementation, per se, this section is perhaps the most ideal place for various examples of QR Code implementations.

This particular letter is more on the no-frills side, but certainly presents itself as a good example of a QR Code implemented with all the right features:

1. *Color is heavily employed, in the franchise's signature hues.*
2. *This is a Unitag (http://unitag.io) QR Code without added embellishment.*
3. *A specific call to action: "Visit or Scan Here…". As always, a clear call-to-action is essential.*
4. *A mobile-friendly landing page (now defunct, as this is an old mailer).*
5. *A human-readable version of the URL, for non-scanners.*
6. *A Query-String Appended QR Code that slightly differs from the main URL, to distinquish scanners from other visitors, for analytics purposes.*
7. *A suggested App download (which, it should be noted, becomes less and less necessary as device manufacturers have added features to their camera apps to automatically recognize and scan the QR Codes – an idea whose time has certainly come, and which tends to obviate the need for this CTA).*
8. *Static QR Code of course does not vary across mailers, and is a part of the art, rather than a confusing add-on.*

Sample Direct Mail Letter Art with QR Code:

1. *QR Code Trademark Info: Sorry DENSO: The trademark words "QR Code" do not appear hereon, so we've foregone the copyright notice. I hate to do it, but often there are already plenty of disclaimers, and this one just adds to the clutter. Call me a hypocrite.*

USE YOUR CHECKS & SAVE OVER $1,000 ON THE SERVICE & UPGRADE OF YOUR VEHICLE.

Dear

While others may just send you impersonal postcards, flashy car flyers or "cut-out" coupon offers that you can't find when you need them, we wanted to show you that we value you by sending something unique, customized and of unprecedented value to set ourselves apart as **your** chosen service center.

THE GIFT THAT KEEPS ON GIVING:
We are very excited to extend to you Quick Lane's® exclusive *"For the Love of Your Car"* program. Enclosed you will find your book of Car Care Checks with more than $1,000 in valuable discounts for the care and maintenance of your vehicle. There are discount checks for savings on oil changes, savings on your regularly scheduled maintenance, and substantial savings for repairs. You're probably due for service right now, but if not, hold on to this VIP checkbook because it doesn't expire until **May 15, 2015**!

OUR GOAL FOR THESE CAR CARE CHECKS:
To give you the VIP treatment you deserve when you service with us. Allow us to give you the VIP treatment *"For the Love of Your Car"* here at Quick Lane®. We are confident that once you experience our superb service, you will become a customer for life.

YOUR SPECIAL MONEY-SAVING VIP OFFERS:
Go ahead and flip through your checkbook now to see the VIP offers we have included especially for you, then call Quick Lane® of Cleveland, your official checkbook redemption center, to book your first appointment.

OUR BONUS PRIZE OFFER:
If you activate your checkbook online within the next 24 hours, you will automatically get a chance in our prize drawing on **May 31st, 2014**. The winner will receive 7 nights of complimentary resort accommodations, with no purchase necessary. It's quick and easy, just go to ***QLC.CarCareChecks.com*** or visit the dealership today! We customized this VIP checkbook just for you, so please take full advantage of it, I look forward to seeing you soon.

Sincerely,

Quick Lane®

Visit or scan here with your phone to activate your check book and register to win!
Don't know how to Scan Yet? Get the app at www.i-nigma.mobi
http://QLC.CarCareChecks.com

Quick Lane® - 1009 US Hwy 59 South - Cleveland, TX 77327 -

2. *The placement is good. No safety concerns or stupidity.*
3. *Text URL is provided for non-scanners (An additional query string is encoded in the matrix to distinguish between typed & scanned visits).*
4. *Explanation: What it does.*
5. *Call to Action: "Scan Here... to win!"*
6. *Recommended App Download: as previously: Use i-nigma (the block is modified from unitaglive.com's default generated version).*
7. *Image Quality: 300 dpi for print, each time, every time.*
8. *Display Size: This one is bigger than needed, in fact. ¾" is plenty.*

9. *Error Correction: Little is required for disposable printed matter.*
10. *Rules: The quiet zone is slightly cramped from the ideal, but not much. The blue bar could get much closer with no issue.*
11. *Direct URL Access: The destination is encoded directly in the QR Code Matrix.*
12. *URL Shortening: Not needed. Note the Short Subdomain: QLC: 3 letters only. This was planned to minimize matrix complexity.*
13. *Friendly URL: The brand's URL is encoded into the QR Code.*
14. *Redirectable URL: This QR Code was intended to be disposable. However, as it encodes a subdomain, as recommended, it can be redirected in minutes to land anywhere.*
15. *Low data density: For a neat & tidy QR-y look and feel.*
16. *Be Secure: The subscription form uses an encrypted SSL connection.*
17. *Tracking: Google Analytics is fully integrated on-site & the convenient query-string mentioned above allows GA to track visits based on scan vs. manual.*
18. *Color & Design. Obviously, full color is key. Take our word for it. View the color version on the website.*
19. *Mobilize: The responsive mini-site adjust to all screen sizes, and was implemented using the flexible multi-site configuration with the Wordpress CMS.*
20. *Proper Function: Truly, this is usually more a function of the underlying website landing page than the QR Code itself.*
21. *Test, Test & Re-Test: Take my word for it. Everything from the flow of website redirects between the subdomain, wildcard subdomain referrer, www. vs. 'naked' subdomain: nothing is left to chance.*
22. *Content is King: The landing page (actually a mobile mini-site) offers users the chance to register for a prize, lookup their make & model vehicle to check for manufacturer recalls, view articles related to car maintenance, download coupons, etc: The more, the better.*
23. *Validation: as a self-appointed QR Code expert, I'm comfortable with the reliability of this QR Code for this application. However, total campaign cost to the client was under $6,000 for this campaign... of which the QR Code's functionality is a small, small part. For a major, national campaign with a seven-figure price tag and perhaps 100x the reach, margins for error narrow, and those excluded by not validating could be in the thousands.*
24. *Make it Social: Note the like & share buttons on the landing page.*
25. *Privacy: No personally-identifiable information is exchanged, except with the secure form.*

18. Security Concerns

There has been much noise made on the side of QR Code detractors, claiming that QR Code technology is not secure enough and creates a significant security risk for scanners. This is irrational and ignorant resistance to something about which they simply have no comprehension. It must be kept in mind that QR Codes are simply bar codes, and can be used to store nearly any data or URL. But, only text data. They simply cannot be used to store viruses or other dangerous material. And yet, serious concerns and overblown rumors seems to constantly circulate, based on isolated incidents and scare tactics, such as:

- *Reports that QR Code scans can result in text message charges being posted to your phone bill.*
- *Reports that QR Codes can be used as a vehicle for downloading viruses that may damage your phone's OS.*
- *Reports that QR Codes can be used as a gateway for stealing your data.*
- *Reports that QR Codes can install Viruses or Malware on your device.*

It's important to note when speaking of QR Codes, that a QR Code is simply a stored URL, in all of these cases… a simple string of text. It's not different than a typed URL, except that it is machine-readable. It is interesting that the same Bloggers are mum as to the dangers of clicking shortened URLs, essentially a game of computer-based Russian roulette. Where is the ultimate destination of a shortened link? That's anyone's guess, and someone who clicks one risks the health of their computer and security of their private information, all at once.

The same applies to anyone who downloads software or files from the Internet from untrusted sources, or simply because the browser told them to.

How many out there, despite the constant warnings, click on shortened links, or any links, simply because they can't help themselves, like little children who must touch the stove to learn, or like Pandora sneaking a peek in the box. These reports are based on several key motivations and factors:

Sensationalistic Pseudo-Journalism:

Sex, Shock & Scares sell newspapers, win Blog readership & Social Media shares. Information doesn't go viral because it was boring. Razor blades found in Halloween candy, infected needles found in cinema seats, the ubiquitous little girl found with her head shaved in a discount store lavatory after her abductor heard the "Code Adam" all-call and fled, mid-abduction. All fiction, and all several years old, but still making their seasonal rounds in chain emails & Social Media shares faster than dogs dancing on two legs and doing the Harlem

Shake. Rock-solid security doesn't often go viral. It's boring. Nothing ever happens.

What does go viral are scares over phones being hijacked, viruses infecting phones, automatic text message sending, billing new charges to cell phones, long distance or for-fee service enrollments, access to contacts, etc, are all scare tactics employed by QR Code detractors. The bottom line is that it requires a great deal of effort, knowledge, research, technique, and experience to write intelligently about how to use a technology properly. It requires just a wild imagination to engage in fear-mongering and "go viral." It is apparent that this is the most common motivation for media that I encounter that is critical of QR Code technology. And this is because of…

Vested Financial Interest of the Writer:

It's true. The Internet today is monetized in ways that would shock and surprise many casual Internet users. Internet content and traffic, as well as Social Media shares and likes are indeed capital of real and quantifiable business value. Many bloggers and internet content writers simply seek to generate content to attract readers, and encourage sharing, promoting click-throughs, generating advertising revenue through banner advertising, pay-per-impression (PPI) display advertising, pay-per-click (PPC) advertising, generating affiliate program sales. As with the sensationalistic print journalism of the past, there is now, as ever, a tenuous balance between good journalism that does a service to those wishing to stay informed and viral journalism that seeks only to be noticed and generate buzz. All-too-often, the scales tip in favor of the latter.

Quick reality check: If you see banner ads, affiliate links, or anything for sale on a site, the owner makes money from visitors, and so has a vested interest in grabbing your attention, stirring the pot, and fear-mongering.

Promoters of Competing Technologies:

Another common thread in much media, particularly online blogs that are critical of QR Code technology comes from owners and marketers of competing technologies. This is discussed in-depth in the later chapter on QR Code Competitors. In a nutshell, because QR Codes are an open technology, anyone is able to create them (for free), direct them to any site (for free), and generally use them any way they please (for free). Further, anyone with a QR Code scanner is able to scan them as well (for free), and browse the content on their choice of device (you guessed it… also completely free).

Many companies have sought to develop proprietary options. These include the Microsoft TAG, Shotcodes, Blotcodes, and other technologies detailed in later chapters, many of which charge a fee for their services, and some of which have extensive legal licensing agreements which must be adhered to, which prohibit certain uses (including free commercial use). *Security* is often listed as a selling point. In reality, the ultimate security of the destination site is the only security issue, and in that they don't differ from QR Codes at all. *Control* and monetization of the technology is the key issue. *Security* is merely a sales pitch.

Read: If everyone one earth only does business with me and my technology, they'll be free from the worry and potential security risk of not knowing who controls the technology... because I will. Hmm. You hear me Microsoft? Shotcodes?

Real Concerns About Security

Let's face it: any device that runs software can run bad software. The main reason that iOS, Android, and Blackberry host their own App Stores is to ensure security, and prevent malicious software from bringing millions of their customers' phones to a screeching halt. Otherwise, any phone will be susceptible to hacking & malicious software. This was a great threat that emerged for phones when they began running Java (one of the first open-source programming languages supported by phone operating systems). As phones become more and more like computers, they will become more susceptible to viruses and malware.

For iOS, to its credit, it's impossible to install any software on an iPhone except from Apple's app store[1]. For Android, unfortunately, as of this writing it is possible for anyone to download a .APK file (Android OS application executable) from anywhere online and install it. Sorry, Android, but sometimes the reputation of your brand depends on taking a stand and telling your customers "NO" when they're too stupid too look after their own safety and use technology responsibly. I'm sorry that's harsh. But, I've spent two decades ignoring "download me" messages, spam emails, porn, p0rn and pr0n offers, and working hard to ensure that I browse safely and take care of my hardware. I have zero sympathy for compulsive downloaders. They're the same as the compulsive chain email forwarders. No. Sympathy.

The Kernel of Truth

I recall listening to a radio station last year, that invited listeners to text "donate" to their five-digit SMS short code, in order to donate $10 to a specific charitable cause. Later that month, I received a $10 charge to my phone bill, just like all other responders to the advertisement... and just like I intended.

There has been a documented case of malware exploiting phone operating systems using SMS short codes. It's essentially the same thing as the above *legitimate* example, except that in the case of Russia (as well as several other Eastern-European countries), all that's necessary to accrue the charge is to send a text to the SMS short code; no confirmation is necessary. And no recourse exists for redress in a country utterly lacking consumer protections.

Notoriously, as reported on Scientific American's website, in September 2011, a Trojan was documented that accompanied an Android ICQ (Internet Chat) application called "Jimm." The URL was a direct link to an APK file, an Android-OS executable, which harbored the Trojan on board. Visitors to the Russian (.ru) site intended to download the free application, and did. The Trojan, in turn, used the application to send SMS messages to Russian SMS short-codes that automatically sign up the user for services, and charge the customers through their phone company on their monthly bill. How were QR Codes to blame? Evidently, some of the downloaders of the Trojan seem to arrived at the site via QR Code scan.

Now, admittedly I may be a devoted QR Code aficionado who is simply not prone to find fault with QR Code technology. Fair enough. But to me, this sounds like a convergence of several problems utterly unrelated to QR Codes, at all:

- *Computer and Mobile Device users foolishly navigating anywhere they please (an ounce of care could prevent this).*
- *Computer and Mobile Device users downloading apps without thinking (there are ugly things out there)*
- *Faults that lie entirely with peculiarities in the Russian telecom billing system (FYI for English-language authors that mention this incessantly… it can't happen in the Western hemisphere)*
- *Poor customer service and advocacy Russian telecom companies (once again, if you're reading the English-language version of this book, you've got nothing to worry about).*
- *Poor legislation and consumer protection in Russia, which clearly seems to favor big business over consumers.*
- *Android OS's lack of quality control and authentication in the App Market. (ie, the ability of Android OS users to directly download and install software from unreliable sources; iOS, for example, requires all downloads through its App store, and other program files cannot be downloaded directly).*

Another often-repeated concern about QR Codes, though never actually documented in practice that I could find, is the fear that scammers might print their own QR Codes on stickers and then stick these QR Codes over the legitimate ones on marketing materials, such as posters. While this is certainly a possibility, I truly hesitate to dignify this myth by addressing it, it would be a rare situation wherein this would have the intended effect, for several reasons:

- *Your Call to Action (a Best Practice, which you must employ) will state why the user should scan, and what content you promise them. When a user sees that the content is wrong, they should be concerned.*
- *Your Plain-Text Alternate Response URL (another best practice), will be present to inform the Users where the link should go.*
- *The visitor should see quite quickly that the URL to which the QR Code scan resolved is not your site.*
- *At some point, people need to take responsibility for their own browsing, downloading and installing practices. Sorry, but they do.*

- *At some point, things are beyond your control. What if, instead of a sticker substituting another QR Code for yours, a scammer chooses to counterfeit your entire poster?*

To draw out this last point, there was a documented case of a company counterfeiting a branch of global electronics giant NEC: not just counterfeit products or theft, but the entire company was counterfeited, complete with branch corporate offices, 50 satellite factories, products of adequate quality, look-alike branding, and a new corporate office setup to do business as the company, as reported on 1 May, 2006 in the New York Times. Signage. Letterhead. An army of employees who thought they worked for NEC, carrying business cards with the company logo.

But is the Problem with QR Codes?

Some things you can guard against and some things you cannot. There is no help for some people who just can't help clicking and downloading everything. And there is nothing to keep a perfectly innocuous-looking URL that is typed or clicked from linking somewhere malicious. I could click the same malicious link from my desktop, phone, or an Internet café in Bangkok. What does that have to do with QR Codes?

Ultimately, there is most certainly the potential for URLs to direct to unsafe locations on the Internet, be it a completely well-intentioned (though virus-infected server), or an actual spoof, phishing, Trojan, or attack site. It would be foolish to think that mobile devices would be entirely immune to virus attacks or deliberate damage. As Smart Phones and other mobile devices (to include iPads, iPods, Kindle & Nook book readers, tablets, etc) have become fully-functioning computers (iOS and Windows Phones run essentially optimized versions of their desktop counterparts), they become just as vulnerable to virus or remote hacking attacks as their larger cousins. The first iPhone, for example, was revolutionary in that it ran the same (albeit somewhat stripped-down and optimized) version of the Mac OSX desktop operating system.

Further, any phones and devices that support Internet browsers essentially run the same web protocols and scripting languages, such as Javascript and Flash (which iOS has never supported in it's on-board phone browsers, citing security reasons).

The Best Defense is Multi-Pronged:

First, if feasible, purchase a website SSL (Secure Socket Layer) Security Certificate from your hosting company. This is a necessary step for many eCommerce sites: most serious online merchant processors, such as Authorize.net and Paypal.com won't share data with you and disable advanced checkout functionality unless you're secure. It's an inexpensive option, adding a layer of much-needed security to your site for every purpose. It is a basic step to safeguard visitors' private information, for any site that collects it. If your site has sufficient functionality to request user information, offer goods for sale, provide contact forms or eCommerce checkout, you should have one to ensure the security of your site for visitors and customers. These aren't expensive. GoDaddy, for example, sends out promotional codes every few days offering them for as little as $10-20 per year (regular price is $69.95), or free with the purchase of services of similar value. If your site runs on it's own server or VPS (Virtual Private Server), your server itself can create it's own self-signed SSL certificate.

However, there's great benefit to purchasing a certificate from a well-known and large certificate authority: More than likely, your visitors will have already visited a site previously and confirmed their acceptance of the SSL authority... and so, they'll be ushered in without delay or security popups.

Second, Brag About It. Display the SSL logo on your website, incorporate the scripts offered by the certificate provider (ie, 'check our security' links), publicize your secure checkout process, and let the scanning public know in clear terms that the ultimate destination of the link they're typing (or the QR Code they're scanning) is a safe place. Real security is an end unto itself, and a laudable goal, but don't forget that our primary concern is two-fold: first making it secure, and equally important, making your customers understand that it's secure for their peace of mind; fear of malicious sites is about a million times more common than actual malicious sites.

Third, use a Friendly URLs (next chapter), or link directly to content on your own site, so that the content is the content expected, in the location expected (your site), to promote credibility and trust. How many of the links in this book might make someone wary, in another environment? But, in this context, you trust the originator, and at least know who it is (and whom to blame for any problems). Believe it or not, this is more than half the battle. Trust is the real issue that might keep your potential QR Code scanning site visitors away.

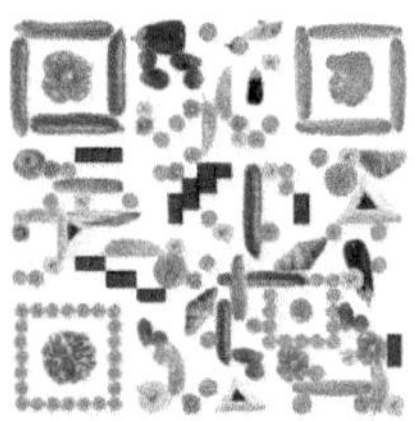

Use Color & Designer Features to add a measure of Counterfeit Protection to your QR Codes.

Fourth, employ Designer QR Codes when possible and practical, as above. Just as U.S. and other currency is chock full of colors, micro-printing, and other security features to make them hard to replicate, you can do the same with your QR Codes; Sound ridiculous? It's not: Using a splash of color, incorporating your logo, and getting a tiny bit creative isn't just a security measure: It's an out-and-out best practice to get the best results from QR Codes, whenever possible.

As has been shown in previous chapters, not only do a splash of color and a company logo work to build your brand, credibility and legitimacy in the most general sense, but further (much like anti-counterfeiting measures taken with currency), they raise the technical bar for potential scammers who might seek to try to insinuate themselves into your campaign. Don't forget that criminals seldom work hard. They aren't going to spend hours meticulously pasting images of tiny tomatoes, cucumbers, and baguettes over the black squares of a QR Code, just to mimic a small catering company's QR Code, divert 30% of scanners (Android users who are vulnerable to malicious .APK files), and net perhaps one accidental victim per month: who may be useless to them, if there's not much the malicious app finds it can do, or the user's settings don't allow it to do dangerous things. So, set the bar too high for a scammer, and they'll find an easier target. The bar doesn't have to be very high. If they weren't the laziest people on earth, they'd get real jobs.

Fifth, also a Best Practice, Provide a Text-Only URL, that users can type to reach the URL without a QR Code scan. Note only does this enable the scanning-impaired consumer to visit your Landing Page as well, but it works in tandem with your QR Code, so that wary consumers will see that the QR Code does indeed resolve to the same URL as is printed on your materials (if you choose to encode a slight variation in your QR Code to distinguish the QR Code scan visitors, base it on this one, or expand a short URL after the scan to add other data).

Sixth, if high-security is truly needed, such as if you're a bank soliciting financial information through the Landing Page, or any application where an extremely large number of visitors are expected (thus, increasing the value for potential scammers), it may indeed be best to opt for a proprietary technology, such as the Shotcode or a Microsoft Tag. With the latter, you not only get the above – an impossible-to-counterfeit proprietary link, with a safe recommended scanning app. And tell your customer to *only* scan with the recommended app.

The Synopsis on Security

Ultimately, from your perspective as the QR Code publisher and implementer, while there is certainly an inherent obligation to minimize reasonable risk for your visitors and customers, the biggest risk present in the vast majority of cases is merely fear on the part of potential consumers who may be concerned about the nature of the content that awaits them on the other side of the QR Code scan. Actual risk from malicious content is very rare, and to be honest, is going to be on someone else's site, not yours. But, nearly every visitor is aware that visiting a website and providing information is risky. Put them at ease. To the extent that you've put effort into making your site more secure, let visitors know.

One Final Note on Security & PII

Please see the note in the advanced strategy discussion on the merits of adding personal data into the URL coded in the QR Code. For the vast majority of implementations, this isn't possible, and the most that would be coded into a QR Code is a tracking code, which isn't *personally identifiable information (PII).*

However, for some use cases – such as dynamic/variable QR Codes for direct mail, and QR Codes generated on-the-fly for online, point-of-sale device display, or other similar situations where a unique QR Code is customized for each consumer, the possibility exists to make a mess.

Protection and accountability for personally Identifiable Information, such as phone, name, email, address, etc, has become a hot-button issue for many U.S. states and localities – and has long been codified in European laws[2]. States such as California, and many others now following suit, are restricting how data can be used, and giving consumers rights concerning how their data is stored and accessed.

Google has been way ahead of this for at least a decade, and the Google Analytics Terms of Service prohibit pushing PII into it's analytics system. Appending PII to URLs necessarily pushes this information into tracking systems of all sorts, and makes it impossible to control the data and allow consumers to opt-out as they desire, putting the operator out of legal compliance.

So, for "generic" (one QR Code for all) implementations, by all means go to town. But, for situations where a QR Code is generated for a unique user to scan – and thereby identify that user and/or track back to that users – or where information to identify that users is coded into the QR Code matrix itself, it is wise to consider the risk/reward balance.

---

[1] *In truth, you could register as an application developer, download Apple's iOS Software Developer Kit (SDK), write an iOS app yourself and install it on your own iPhone. But, in that case, we can all fairly say that you are responsible for any faulty code. Want to load malicious software on your own device? Have fun. But, the point here is that you can't publish or circulate it. It's safe.*

[2] *In fact, within the European Union, it has long been the practice to obfuscate IP addresses for privacy reasons, to prevent the sort of pin-point location information that many advertisers and web applications rely on. This sort of obfuscation has only in very recent years been adopted in the U.S. by device manufacturers and browser publishers.*

19. Friendly URL Hosting

Speaking of stupid people clicking anything they see, I received a Twitter direct message, one memorable day in mid-2012 from a friend that I know very well, and inside the message was *"This is exactly what you were asking me about the other day!"* followed by a shortened URL. Without thinking, I clicked on the shortened link (which used the goo.gl shortener). Any guesses as to what sort of perversions exploded onto my massive computer screen?

A XXX-rated slideshow gallery montage of video snippets & full-motion animated image thumbnails, thrusting and bouncing and writhing across my screen in a perverse competition, each vying to be more despicable than the next (and each winning, in its own uniquely disturbing way), grunting and moaning through my computer speakers at maximum volume, building and harmonizing in an unholy crescendo: a symphony of vice that could only have been composed by the Emperor Caligula himself.

I fumbled for the volume control and quickly closed the window before turning my desk chair around, standing up, and peeking out my office door for witnesses. Finding none, I returned to my desk, took a deep breath, and contacted my friend, whose Twitter account had of course been hacked, and who had sent the same link to everyone he knows. Or the email was a Twitter notifier spoof and it wasn't really him. Who knows. I didn't really care to launch into full-on network forensics mode. It happens. Just not to me, thanks to my 18-character alphanumeric passwords with assorted non-English symbols & punctuation… and a bit of luck, knock on wood.

But, it could happen to anyone, and believe me, having to apologize to friends and family makes it worth taking a little extra effort to lock things up (including your employees, valued customers, bosses, CEO, Commanding Officer, parole officer, priest, pastor, rabbi, spouse, mother, daughter, or grandmother).

Despite being violations of the terms of service of these URL shorteners, these shorteners are being abused on a massive level by spammers hoping to generate as much traffic as possible. They even seek to trick those disinterested in their wares into clicking through and seeing their products, and hopefully sticking around to buy. URL shorteners are a way of concealing the content until it's too late to decline; and, because the destination URL isn't revealed until the link is loading, it isn't possible to judge the URL by it's site name, which may be completely obscured or unrelated to the content anyway:

Bit.ly/Fun4Children

might well resolve to…

DisturbingRaunchyPornos.com

Now, this is really just a treatment of a single one of the sources of shortened link spam. There are of course dozens of others, to include the usual suspects, as well as phishing sources:

- *As noted, Porn, P0rN & of course, Pron*
- *"Discounted," Generic, or Brand-Name Prescription Medications*
- *Mortgage and Auto Loan Refinancing*
- *[COUNTERFEIT] Handbags, Fine Watches, or Designer Goods*
- *Phishing scams disguised as notification from Banks, Social Media accounts, etc.*
- *Websites of PPC & PPI marketers who are paid based on how many times their pages load (and ads are displayed for visitors).*
- *Similar affiliate marketing 'professionals' who just need to get some bodies through the gate, to hopefully make some cash later.*

Oddly, over the past few years, unwanted "ambush porn" has largely been curtailed. I can't remember the last time I was suckered by that one. But, it's been replaced by an army of spam to replace it – arguably more disruptive:

- *Solar energy offers*
- *Automotive service plans/fake warrantees*
- *Healthcare plan offers*
- *Business financing, merchant capital, and factoring*
- *Credit card processing services*
- *Real estate agent spam*

And of course, this doesn't even begin to address the truly bad sites that will attempt to install malware, spyware, and do real damage to your computer system. Where am I going with this?

Build Trust in Your Links and QR Codes

This is a more detailed treatment of the Friendly Hosting concept, as discussed in the previous chapter on general security. As QR Codes become more and more mainstream, and awareness continues to grow (and URL Shorteners continue to be abused), consumers will be less and less enthusiastic about typing a random, shortened URL into their browsers, whether from phone or desktop. I won't do it again.

Using a Bit.ly or a Goo.gl shortened URL doesn't inspire confidence, as they are free and anyone, anywhere is able to use them to shorten as many of any type of URL as they like. Further, they certainly don't do anything to build your brand identity. Perhaps your customers simply trust you and will click or scan anything you throw at them. But, more than likely, they will eventually come to think twice, particularly the market segments that are most vulnerable to malicious code and potential abuses.

Friendly URL Hosting is the Answer

My recommendation is something I like to call *Friendly URL Hosting.* Why Friendly? It's the opposite of a stranger. You know a friend by name and reputation. Therefore, whenever possible, host your content directly on your site, so that those scanning your QR Code can have confidence in knowing that they are visiting your site, and aren't about to risk being steered into the debacle into which I was steered. How can this be done?

Just Host it Yourself

The single, best solution is to host the content and destination for your QR Code scan on your own site, with your own company's URL. However, this may be difficult, as your current site may not be mobile optimized (see Chapter 9 for ideas for mobilizing your site). As discussed there, simple alternatives to fully mobile-optimizing your site can be using a responsive website design (that adjusts to the visitor's screen size) or creating simple Landing Pages to direct your visitors who arrive by QR Code scan.

There are, of course, serious limitations to this technique, since it generally ups the ante of the technical ability that will be required of you: Without an intermediate stop created by a shortener, it becomes more technically demanding to track response and count visitors. Adding analytics and visitor tracking coding to your web pages will be essential It can be done quite easily with Google Analytics, but a tiny pinch of web development savvy will be needed.

It's very easy to use a QR Code to link directly to a YouTube video directly, but a YouTube link is precisely the sort of anonymous link that might cause visitors to balk. The preferred alternative is embedding the video directly on your site.

And customer confidence isn't the only reason for such a move. Sending prospects, leads and potential customers to your own site provides a more "sticky" user experience (keeping them on your own site), rather than on Youtube, where they can get distracted by dancing dogs and falling cats and Charlie biting his brother's finger, Charlie the Unicorn complaining about his stolen liver, the Ultimate Harlem Shake compilation du jour, ten thousand amateur covers of the latest Lady Gaga song, Karman's riot of a cover of "Look at me Now," or any number of random distractions that nearly a billion users have agreed is more engaging than your marketing message, and forget what they're doing, wandering off, probably never to return.

So, keep the Landing Pages on your site, and keep the customers on your site. If video hosting is what you need, embed the videos, while hosting them on Youtube, and be sure to disable the "suggested videos" feature: watching other people's videos unrelated to your message while on your site is an improvement over totally losing them entirely to Youtube, but it's still not ideal.

Hosting via a CDN (Content Delivery Network) is another option. Using Vimeo.com rather than Youtube allows you to allow embedding only from your site: The content can't be used elsewhere. Thus, your content only promotes your site.

A full-fledged CDN like Amazon S2 can be used as well; setup is fast and you can upload videos or any content to be served up on demand by Amazon's ultra-solid infrastructure... securely, without the risk of others embedding your content.

Create a Separate Mobile Website

This can be done easily by using any of the providers described in Chapter 9. Ideally, these sites will provide a short snippet of website code that you'll add to your website's pages, which will intercept mobile visitors and re-direct them to the mobile version of your site. While this is always a great idea, there's nothing to say you have to do this, if it's beyond your technical abilities. You could also simply treat the mobile site as a stand-alone site, and direct your mobile traffic to it directly, by coding the direct link to the site as the destination URL for your QR Code. Ideally, it would be great if your entire website was mobile optimized. But, for our purposes, it's enough just to have your QR Code Landing Pages optimized. For this purpose, it doesn't matter where they're hosted. Just code your QR Code with the URL. Even better…

Do it on a Subdomain of Your Website

That means something like this:

`https://subdomain.website.com`

This will keep the URL short, friendly, and promote your own website. This will take some minor doing through your Hosting service's hosting control panel, but is no more difficult than other options. When you set up your subdomain through your web hosting company's hosting control panel, indicate the URL of the mobile site you created as the URL the Domain Name Server should deliver.

If you choose to do this, be sure to read the articles on the Blog at Eshlepper.com, specifically "*The Google Reflex*" and "*A Record & C Name Shenanigans*," which are two easily-resolvable challenges when using Landing Pages, and subdomains in particular. In most ways, as detailed elsewhere herein, a subdomain is superior to any other option for hosting a Landing Page for your QR Code scanning visitors. Whereas a specific webpage adds substantial length to your URL, a subdomain may consist of perhaps a single letter, making it http://q.YourWebsite.com, which makes mobile site visitors at home, while preserving a Short, Friendly URL. Visitors are also prone to stop typing at ".com", and have in fact developed the muscle reflex of hitting return after typing ".com". So, putting a subdomain on the front end makes them less prone to forget to type the "slug" or page name.

Do it With a CMS

While learning to write HTML, CSS, PHP, jQuery, Javascript, ASP.NET, MySQL, and other programming and scripting languages is difficult and time-consuming, it's easy to host amazing sites with a Content Management System (CMS) such as Wordpress, Joomla, or Drupal installed. I recommend Wordpress. Wordpress is very easy to use and quite powerful (in fact, I've built many client websites using Wordpress), including the Eshlepper.com companion site to this book. Basic features can help get a total novice set up in just a few minutes, and with practice, nearly any level of advanced web programming is possible, simply by selecting (mostly free) plugins and applying (again, mostly free) themes. Further, you can easily create near-infinite Landing Pages, and give each a short, descriptive name, called a "slug," which makes navigation a snap.

While it's possible to completely replace (or build from scratch) your current website with a Wordpress site, most likely that's not something you're ready to consider. If you're only interested in some mobile optimized pages, you can install Wordpress in a subdirectory or subdomain of your existing site, and use it only for your Landing Pages, Blog, or to add some marketing automation to your business. Just select a template ("theme") that is Mobile Optimized (search for a "Mobile," or "Responsive" template to find one that automatically adjusts to the visitor's screen size and device) and keep it simple, because it's still possible to overdo it.

There are hundreds of free themes available at Wordpress.org for download (or browse, download, install and activate them directly through your Wordpress installation). I've used a number of themes for this, including, "Mio", "Ward", and others. *Ward* is great, out of the box, with a simple, clean, "flat" design that scales well to mobile screens and works perfectly for a landing page for offers or information. Alternately, premium themes can be purchased all over the Internet for anywhere from $30-150. My recommendations are as follow:

www.TemplateMonster.com: Recommended. Amazing themes for all CMS systems, and even standalone sites and landing pages. Some of the nicest themes I've seen and purchased have been from here. Great support. The only site I've encountered that delivers sites as demonstrated (ie, looking like the demos). But fair warning: due to the nature of Wordpress, getting this effect requires some back-end surgery and familiarity with the system. If that's not you, pay for an install.

www.ElegantThemes.com: Recommended. Get access to their entire library of gorgeous themes for $69... barely $1 each. Archive for later.

www.ThemeForest.com: This is a prominent site online, run by an Australian company called Envato. Expect to overpay for anything you purchase. Their pricing scheme requires prepayment of a deposit to an account, from which money for purchases are drawn; Expect to find that the down payments you make leave multiples of $5 on deposit with their company, requiring a second purchase to use it. Also expect to be hit with a 3% international payments surcharge by your bank. OK. Now that you're aware that you'll be hustled for at least an extra $5-15 that you won't be able to spend on a single purchase, and stuck with an international funds transfer surcharge, and are walking in with eyes wide open...

The site has potential. Purchase individual landing pages, images, scripts, themes and templates, ranging from $1-5 for an image or a code snippet, application plugin, theme.

www.Themify.me: No recommendation. Access to several dozen themes for $79; 30-day trial with a refund guarantee. Sold!

www.SimpleThemes.com: Get access to the entire library for 3-months for $49. Bear in mind that the fee is primarily for help & support, as many of the themes are free in general, and several are in fact downloadable and installable directly through Wordpress from the theme library for free.

Wordpress is available as a free download at http://www.wordpress.org, so you can install it on any site you control, by simply following the instructions (*See Chapter 9 for more information on Wordpress features and plugins*). Further, most large hosting services allow you to automatically install Wordpress for free, with just a few clicks through their hosting control panel, including the following hosting services:

- *Host Gator http://www.hostgator.com*
- *Blue Host: http://www.bluehost.com*
- *GoDaddy: http://www.godaddy.com*
- *1and1: http://www.1and1.com*
- *Any server installation of Cpanel or PLESK.*
- *And many, many more.*

Host Your Own Friendly URL Shortener

Another of my favorite solutions is to host my own URL shortener via a fantastic program I've found called YOURLS, Your Own URL Shortener. YOURLS can also be downloaded free of charge, set up with minimal Web Development know-how (also automatically by some hosting services, such as the above list), and adds a touch of style and unique branding to your website short links. GoDaddy actually has the YOURLS application ready for automatic installation for hosting customers, as may others.

Bit.ly, the ubiquitous URL shortener, can be integrated with your website as well. Simply provide a (preferably short) URL, perform the setup (complete instructions at the Bit.ly site), and you're ready to go, with all the performance and functionality of the Bit.ly system, run through your own site, under your own name, for consistent branding.

The Summary:

Make sure that the links displayed let your visitors know that it's YOU, and not some creep out there to steal their information. This is a no-brainer: kill several birds with one stone: it's about *trust, security, branding, prestige & status*. Brand your site.

20. QR Code Competitors

There are a number of technologies that currently vie for the QR Code's position as the go-to technology for print-to-digital media linking. But, given the complete and total dominance of QR Codes, it is probably inaccurate to call their attempts "vying"; QR Codes are completely dominant in every market, and have become ubiquitous. Below is a more or less complete sampling of the competing technologies vying for dominance with QR Codes. Perhaps I overstate the scope of competition. QR Codes are the dominant technology. Most likely, you may have seen a Microsoft Tag or two at some point. The others will no doubt be completely foreign to you. I've never seen any of them in the wild. Not a single one. And I looked.

Some other codes, such as PDF417, Dotcode and Data Matrix simply aren't seeking to be the popular marketing tool that QR Codes have become. Dotcodes have been relegated to use for the United Parcel Service (UPS) in tracking shipping items. Datamatrix seems stuck in industrials settings. PDF417 or some analogy made an appearance on some mobile Pass applications. The major ones seem to have found their roles.

Few of these technologies have any actual functional benefit over QR Codes, and all have an immensely reduced ability to store data. In fact, the single most key attribute that all these varying technologies have in common is the lack of data storage; in most cases, just a few bytes or dozen bytes. Essentially, this is precisely enough to store a shortened URL, which is what they store. Just an index number used to look up the URL in ***their own exclusive*** proprietary database.

Proprietary vs. Open Technology:

Aside from the lack of storage, the main factor that sets these technologies apart, is that (as opposed to QR Codes), they are proprietary, patented technologies. They aren't "open." What this means is that marketers & business owners (like you and me) aren't free to use the technology to generate our own codes, nor are we free to use them as we please. This has stymied and slowed their acceptance, and will probably limit the development of the technologies permanently. Whereas the Denso-Wave corporation has given the green light to the world to develop it's QR Code technology and use it free, the creators of these other codes insist on controlling their creations, licensing it as they please, subject to their terms, charging a premium for commercial use, and reserving the right to police the use of the codes, changing fees in the future as they please, and perhaps rendering codes unreadable, retroactively. It doesn't lend itself to creating a feeling of confidence in the consumer (you and me), nor of stability and trust that the codes will be useful, economical, or even available in the future. For example, the Shotcode Terms of Service, available at Shotcode.com, specifically contraindicate commercial use, specify suspension of use for "abuse," and reserve the right to charge in the future. It also requires a substantial legal licensing agreement to use. In short, it's made clear that Shotcodes are not yours to do with as you please, but rather, remain the intellectual property of their owner, in perpetuity. You may only use them at their pleasure, until they decide otherwise, whereupon every piece of material on which you may have affixed a Shotcode must be destroyed or surrendered, and cannot be legally used due to trademark infringement (they export with a "Shotcode™" attached.

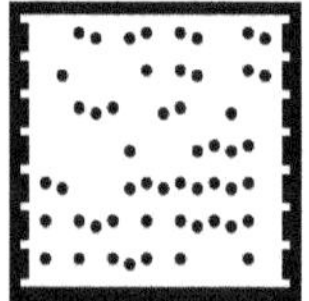

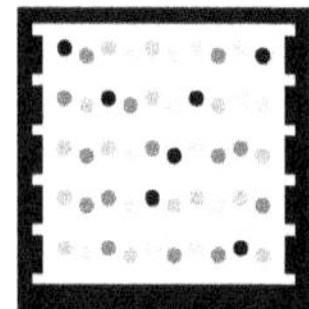

How would they "render the codes unscannable?" Quite simply, all of these schemes differ from QR Codes in that they do not store (nor do they have the data storage capacity to store) the actual coded data in the matrix itself. Instead, they store only a proprietary identifier. When scanned, the identifier is matched with the data stored on the company's server, and the URL (or other info) is served up to the mobile user's browser. Should they ever decide to disable the lookup process for your codes, that's that. This is analogous to using a URL shortener with your QR Codes: instead of the actual data, just a short link to the real data is stored. Now imagine that you could only use one URL shortener, forever, and should they change their terms of service, you'll need to cease using your QR Codes forever. This presents several issues:

With a QR Code, you have choice in using a shortening service: as detailed elsewhere in this book, you may use Google's, Bit.ly's (or install Bit.ly's on your own domain), QRstuff's shortener, UniTagLive.com's shortener, or any of a million (literally, a million) URL shorteners for your shortcodes. You can even host your own shortener just for your own use (for free) using the YOURLS self-hosted URL shortener, as I've suggested, download any of hundreds of full-featured scripts to use to create a URL shortener of your own, or write your own URL shortener. Anyone with a bit of PHP/Javascript programming know-how could do it in an hour. Or, if you don't want to shorten? Opt out; encode the URL directly into the QR Code matrix and eliminate the shortener entirely.

With a proprietary code? You're stuck. No options. Forever. With any of these services, you're locked in permanently. You can't change services, host elsewhere, etc. It's as if you were permanently committed, in advance, to a single service, without the ability to change at any time in the future, ever. Monopolies are never good for the consumer.

There is no capacity for storing the actual URL in the code. Access to the codes (ie, whether they scan or not) is permanently dependent on using the given company's server to decode them, including paying any fees they determine to charge now or in the future, intermediate advertising pages they decide to add in the future, their prior approval of your content, as well as the right to determine abusive use and disconnect your service at will.

At least for the time being, support for these technologies is nearly non-existent. Microsoft's Tag reader is the only reader capable of reading Tags (and will remain so, unless the technology is licensed and paid for). Blotcode's proprietary reader is the only one capable of reading theirs, and as for the Shotcodes, there is no current support for iPhone (iOS), Android, Blackberry, or Windows. Their site lists a lengthy list of phones supported, but none of the Big Four are among them. That leaves me scratching my head, since we established earlier in this book that these are the four operating systems doing all the QR Code scanning (and presumably would do other scanning). I was able to produce the below Shotcode for this book, and scan it using Blotcode's recommended reader. Blotcode's scan App claims to be able to do so, but from my experience this is just a claim.

Similarly, awareness of these technologies by consumers is also nearly non-existent, with the notable exception of the Microsoft Tag, which still is barely popular enough to make it onto the radar.

Microsoft Tag

http://www.gettag.mobi Aside from being visually very different from a QR Code, it bears mentioning that the Tag is the number two technology in this game, trailing the QR Code (though by a massive margin). In the course of writing this entire book, I only encountered two Microsoft Tags, including the one at right that I generated just for this chapter. In fact, while researching this book, I was hard-pressed to actually find a live one to scan, the only one being for a local dental office.

This is most likely due to a combination of factors, including the Tag's relatively new entrance into the marketplace, as well as the proprietary nature of the Tag technology; Only Microsoft Tag users can create them, and only the MS Tag App can scan them. Since the technology belongs to the Microsoft Corporation, it is subject to numerous controls and proprietary obstacles to widespread adoption & acceptance. As mentioned numerous times elsewhere, the 'open-source' nature of QR Codes and the refusal of DENSO-WAVE to enforce their copyright has contributed greatly to the proliferation of QR Codes.

Moreover, the QR Code is an older, more mature, and better established technology, so expect to see more Microsoft Tags in the future. The benefits of the Microsoft Tag are many.

- *First and foremost, their application and online dashboard support both QR Code generation and scans as well as their proprietary Tag technology, to their great credit. Their app can be the only app on a mobile device.*
- *The tag is also visually very interesting, and has alternate forms.*
- *Anyone can create Tags for free (subject to Terms of Service), simply by signing in with their Microsoft Live ID.*
- *The Tags have an alternate format, pictured here, which can be overlaid on images, instantly making them scannable. This is a notable feature that excels the other technologies. The custom code can be downloaded as layer files for popular image processing suites (Adobe Photoshop, or Illustrator for example), and overlaid on a logo or image, something that generally cannot be done well with a QR Code without some measure of image processing expertise.*
- *The Microsoft Tag website has extensive downloadable support documentation, including Best Practices for implementing Tags and QR Codes alike, Tips & Tricks, as well as Ideas and general instructions, which are worth downloading and reviewing (as well as implementing), regardless of the code technology you choose.*
- *The Tags can be optionally downloaded with a standard Call to Action, explanation, and URL for downloading the app, one of my recommended Best Practices.*
- *The Tag setup dialog gives the user creating the tag (as well as the person scanning it using the mobile app) the ability to decide whether linked content is opened in the Mobile Device's browser, or in the Tag app directly – a unique feature. This is an annoying difference from other scanning apps, which arbitrarily determine whether to open content in the app or open it in the user's browser (some scanning apps offer this option too, and may override it).*
- *The online code generator platform is already NFC-ready, and can output them in a format ready to code onto your own NFC media.*

The multi-color dots that encode a Microsoft TAG are the forerunners of the future of QR Code technology; whereas today we have 2D barcodes, modulating the color of individual areas within the code is being explored as a means of creating 3D bar codes (color as a third dimension). Even just using the 256 most basic colors, read "8-bit", this could increase the storage capacity of QR Codes and similar technologies beyond imagination, enabling for example, the storing of an entire book in the actual QR Code, or perhaps a minute or so of audio, or dozen images.

For black and white applications, there are black & white options, so that color printing need not drive up the production cost of your project needlessly; the color version certainly will not scan properly if printed in black & white or grayscale[1].

Wimo Reality Triggers:

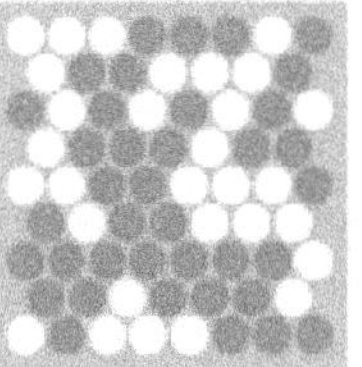

Figure 19

Wimo Trigger

Wimo Reality takes a completely different approach than others, and is perhaps the most sophisticated system out there. It is a proprietary system, a closed system, seeking only high-dollar corporate clients, which limited my ability to investigate their offerings. In short, there is no option to register for free and start using their platform. Which is fine, since none of the readers of this book will be in that elite or have the budget to hire them. However, Wimo's concept is the next step in the print-to-web link paradigm. Wimo incorporates three separate systems in its code scanner and campaigns, each or all of which can be used to link to online content when scanned with Wimo's scanner application:

- *Wimo's proprietary "Trigger" codes, as pictured above, which are certainly more visually interesting than black & white codes, and customizable for any color scheme (including black & white or grayscale if you so desire).*
- *Standard Bar Code Scans for basic 1-Dimensional product UPC bar codes, the unique benefit here being that all packaging already bears them, an excellent touch for a company that would like to adopt the program without making packaging updates – the UPC barcode is the "trigger", and the image of the barcode itself links to other content.*
- *Image recognition technology (without markup or embedded code) can also be used to recognize a company logo, product packaging, or even turn an entire magazine or newspaper article (or portion thereof) into a scannable link.*

The primary benefit of using image-recognition solutions for print-to-web links is to compete with various other technologies that offer image search capability. Examples include Amazon's mobile shopping application, which can scan a UPC bar code or process a photo taken of an item, looking it up, and presenting listings of the item for purchase. From a consumer's perspective (or from Amazon's), this can be very convenient, as an identical item can be purchased immediately with a click or two, on the fly.

However, from the perspective of the product manufacturer, this can be distressing, as a curious consumer is directed to purchase the item from a random retailer, or the one who created the app. Thus, they are denied the opportunity to present their own marketing message, directly track interest, or interact with the consumer directly; essentially, this process circumvents the product manufacturer entirely.

Wimo's push is less to compete with QR Codes, although that is certainly a goal, and more aimed at intercepting these image-recognition searches, directing them to manufacturer-owned online resources, rather than those of another application's publisher. As image search is entering the mainstream, Wimo seeks to capture back these consumers for their clients. Another related factor to consider is that, depending on the type of product, a direct purchase may not be the best option or in the best interest of the manufacturer, in which case a direct search for products online isn't appropriate. For example:

- *For general brand advertising and reinforcement, a purchase isn't the immediate goal, but rather maintaining top-of-mind awareness of the product.*
- *For links from the product packaging itself, whether logo, UPC, or tagged, information on where to purchase is irrelevant: The person scanning it is now holding the product in their hand, either in their home or store. It is the producer's information they need, not an alternate purchase location (from the producer's perspective).*
- *Food items (to include restaurants & fast-food), grocery items, perishable items, toiletries, and such consumer goods are not likely to be purchased online, nor even be available online. A manufacturer-controlled media channel allows content to be tailored to the product type and intended customer demographic.*
- *Clothing, shoes, and similar items that are less likely to be purchased directly online, where fit is a concern, or for designer items where Lifestyle Advertising is preferred.*
- *Movie or theater tickets, especially months before release, are also unlikely to be purchased online immediately. Links are best directed to various online trailers & promotions, etc, to build interest & curiosity.*
- *High-dollar items & items that are simply not available via mail-order, such as cars & trucks, boats, etc, in which sales materials to educate the potential buyer & build excitement, as well as capture contact information, should be preferred.*
- *Services (whether brick & mortar) or online, which would not be subject to immediate purchase, but where a seller would be expected to research several services first.*

If there's any takeaway from meditating on the concept, it comes down to a single key factor: major brands that do business through distributors may have a vested interest in re-inserting themselves into the marketing process downstream a bit. Direct marketing organizations likely have other interests. That definitely makes this an option for the former; in Wimo's words from it's own website:

> *"The brand controls the calls to action and content associated with its image."*

The proprietary trigger markings are attractive & visually interesting, and the process of scanning with Wimo's app is straightforward. However, many that I've scanned failed to properly resolve to their intended destination. Other performance is spotty. For example, scanning the logo on the label of the Coca-Cola bottle on my desk resolved to a video for a new television series about an alien invasion, with a number of other sponsors… but Coke was not among them. Other attempts at scanning random product logos failed to resolve at all (expected, since they couldn't all be WimoReality customers). In a string of tests, the General Electric, Dove Chocolate, Snickers, Oreo Logos, as well as the Zero Vitamin Water logo promoted on WimoReality's website as a client all failed to scan.

This highlights a key point as the print-to-digital link field expands, becoming increasingly dependent on image recognition technology: it becomes more and more difficult to determine what and where a consumer should try to scan. As if it wasn't difficult getting a consumer to recognize a QR Code… now *anything* could be scannable. That flies in the face of the Best Practice of a Call to Action: Scan Here Now. Consumers aren't going to scan everything, in the hopes of something yielding a video or hidden message. When I was eight years old, I spent an entire summer playing the original Legend of Zelda video game on the Nintendo Entertainment System; walking my tiny Link character around the kingdom of Hyrule slaying Peahats and gambling with the man in the cave to win Rupees, buy bombs, and meticulously bomb every block in the entire land of Hyrule, on a mission to find hidden items. Consumers aren't going to do that.

Because of the large client focus, as well as the proprietary nature of Wimo's technology, Wimo markers are not in widespread use, and certainly don't have the acceptance and popularity of QR Codes. And, unlike Microsoft's Tag, which to its credit supports QR Code scans along with their own proprietary technology, Wimo does nothing with QR Codes, which is currently the dominant technology by a landslide, which makes their application fairly useless. Why would a consumer download a dedicated application, solely to interact with Wimo Triggers, when they are so rare in the marketplace? Wimo should have taken a page from the Microsoft Tag playbook (MS seems to be learning from mistakes) and supported the QR Code as well.

Marketing an app with QR Code scan capabilities would seem a far better idea: As QR Codes are the dominant technology, users could use Wimo's scanner as the go-to device for all uses. Unfortunately, in an attempt to supplant QR Codes, they reduce the market for their application. This necessarily presents a problem: a second app is required in order to scan multiple types of codes. For all these reasons, it seems that Wimo's service is ill-conceived and geared for the benefit of manufacturers & brands exclusively. And I can't see much utility in it for them, either.

Shotcodes, Blotcodes & Dandelions:

A Shotcode & Blotcode

While visually very appealing, as compared to QR Codes, especially the Blotcode, which has stolen my heart away, looking like some alien marking from a sci-fi movie, which inspired my *Bubble* designer QR Code frame in Chapter 11), both of these technologies have terribly inadequate data storage capabilities. The Shotcode can store a mere 40 bits of data, and the Blotcode a total of 32 bits of data (essentially 4 and 5 characters, respectively), not even enough for a simple URL, phone number, or really anything at all of use.

Compare that to the QR Code's storage capacity of 4,972 bytes of data (approximately 500-1,000 times greater). Because of this limitation, the actual data encoded cannot be stored in the printed code itself, as it is in a QR Code. Rather, only a proprietary short code of a few digits is stored in the actual matrix of the code.

When the code is scanned, the scanning application contacts the proprietary web server, looks up the full URL for the short code, and then displays the content of that page. The problem with this scheme is that in order for Shotcodes or Blotcodes to function, access to this one, single server (controlled by the publisher) is required, and clearly in order for it to work for every user, there can only be one server... theirs; hence, the drawback of every proprietary technology: everyone else is crowded out of the market. Which works great for the one guy holding all the keys and calling the shots. For the other 7,999,999,999 of us? Not so very attractive.

There is no option for anonymous use. Shotcode.com requires registration, and a legal agreement to use their site, and makes it clear that it may deny access to their database for lookups in the future, and reserves the right to charge. In effect, it's like using a QR Code with a mandatory shortening service – you can only use the owner's URL shortener, not your own or not a competitor's, and you certainly can't store in it what you want. Just a short link[2]. On the same vein, despite my admiration for bit.ly, or even my own shortening solutions, I would reject any options that bound me to one. I'll use all, some or none, thank you very much.

Further, for Shotcodes at least, each comes pre-branded with Shotcode.com's URL printed on each Shotcode generated. This may be beneficial for the consumer in finding out where to get a scanning app (since it is *very difficult)*, and building Shotcode's market share, but for the marketer printing it on his materials, it has limited value and distracts from your message.

I've yet to see a Shotcode in the wild, much less a Blotcode. Period. They're like unicorns. I can't help but wonder if they actually exist. As if this wasn't dismal enough news, there isn't currently any support for iPhone, Android, Windows or Blackberry phones, the current leaders when it comes to QR Codes. Totally neglecting not one, but all of the major smart-phone operating systems leaves me scratching my head. The major thrust of Shotcodes seems to be the international market, and their website is rife with clues that it was assembled overseas (the same applies to Blotcodes). Could it be that Shotcodes are simply not meant for the North American market? I was able to find only one scanner (the recommended one for Blotcodes, 2DSense) app in the iPhone app store, which was able to scan the Blotcode, but although it claims to be capable of Shotcode scans, I could not scan the one I created.

Near Field Communication (NFC)

Near-Field Communication differs substantially from all of these other types of technologies, but is often discussed as a "replacement" for any or all of the above, QR Codes in particular. However, it is simply nothing of the sort. QR Codes, Microsoft Tags, and every other protocol discussed herein are all designed to facilitate print-to-web linking, to display graphic links on printed material that link to online and digital media.

Some of the most common, well-established uses that would be very familiar to consumers include:

- *Retail theft prevention (included as a concealed sticker within compact discs, video discs, small high-value items, hidden within garments, packaging, or on a plastic fob attached to items)*
- *Fast checkouts at the supermarket or gas station; several companies (Texaco's SpeedPass, for example) allows a special card to be waved at the NFC scanner at the checkout station or gas pump to bill fuel purchases to a linked credit card.*
- *Motor vehicles that automatically unlock when the key fob comes within the vicinity of the vehicle (or refuse to lock the doors from the outside if the keys are detected in the car), or push-button start vehicles that require no key insertion at all, or micro-chipped keys that cannot be copied, etc; a scanner embedded in the steering column disables the ignition unless it detects the proper microchip-embedded key.*
- *Security access badges that are scanned to unlock doors.*
- *Pet "microchips" implanted under the skin of a household pet, which can be read by a scanner and searched in a database to retrieve the name and address of the pet owner.*

The list goes on and on. NFC has been around for a while, as RFID. But, as a marketing product, NFC is a brand new concept. The operating theory is that mobile users will use NFC-enabled devices to read NFC "Touch-Points" that contain the RFID transponders, which resolve to URLs to be displayed in the mobile device's browser.

NFC is a completely different and unique technology with completely different uses and capabilities (some of which potentially overlapping -- hence comparison), although there are several uses for which they have been paired.

It is vital to understand that Near-Field Communication is not a printed code that is scanned optically, but rather an embedded radio device, consisting of a tiny microchip and antenna, much akin to the RFID (Radio Frequency ID) tags that are widely used today.

So, it needs to be emphasized that NFC is based on the use of an embedded Radio transponder, which must be concealed within, molded into, or attached to the object that is used as an NFC Touch Point. Thus, it isn't suitable for any printed applications, where ink is simply printed on paper, nor online or televised display, or any applications where the URL may be subject to change, because once the NFC media is ordered, coded, and delivered, it is fixed (subject to potential back-end redirection or recoding as is done with URL shorteners). The RFID module also, though being fairly tiny, does have dimensions, albeit, very meager ones, so they won't be suitable for purposes where the media must be very flat and uniform, such as simple paper, mass-produced posters, mail pieces, etc.

Further, and equally vital to emphasize, the mobile device used to read the Touch Point must have NFC capabilities; a dedicated transmitter is required. Typical phones now will need to have a wireless telephone radio, a Wi-fi data radio for internet access, a Bluetooth radio for the accessories, and now an NFC transmitter/receiver for NFC purposes. So, rather than an onboard app, it requires actual new hardware.

Although in marketing and many uses, this is represented as akin to QR Codes, it is similar only in *apparent use*: the user *appears* to pull out their phone and handle it near the mark. But the similarity is an illusion. Actually, a digital radio communication protocol, similar to Bluetooth and Wi-Fi, is at play. The process is nothing similar. As of publication, there are only a handful of devices that support NFC (Android is the first major manufacturer to embrace).

Initially, NFC didn't seem to have any practical advantages over other technologies at present, since it was not yet well supported. From the user's perspective, scanning a code is essentially no different from waving their mobile device at a Touch Point, which in all cases looks the same as a code scan, and is typically used simultaneously alongside QR Codes or other technologies for response. Indeed, many existing NFC Touch Points are used in tandem with QR Codes, linking the two technologies at least conceptually. In the future, however since major manufacturers are beginning to include NFC technology in phone and mobile device hardware, once it catches on and the majority of phones support it, it will be a standard all its own, independent of the user's selection of application or technology (ie, QR Code vs. Wimo Trigger vs. Microsoft Tag vs. Shotcode), and will be universal.

One possible advantage is that in many cases, the object in which the Touch Point is embedded will have a known location, which cannot be readily duplicated, shared, or copied by other mobile users, so all traffic generated can be traced back to the physical location of the Touch Point. Although unique QR Codes (or other codes) can be uniquely coded to create this effect, it is always possible for the link itself to be shared, making subsequent, secondary traffic resulting from the shared (or bookmarked) link appear as if it was generated by a scan, when in fact, it could be bookmarked, or shared via Social Media or email, just like any URL.

Drawbacks include added expense & turnaround time. Services are already beginning to support NFC (Microsoft's Tag creation site already allows creation of NFC URLs for coding). However, they must be custom-coded with the correct data, as well as shipped to your location, applied to the appropriate media, etc. Since it is in fact a physical object, that is, a recordable piece of media being created, purchased, coded, shipped, and embedded, additional costs will be a given, both for creating, recording, ordering shipping, and handling the media, but also for applying and installing the media. The costs for the media are modest, and will certainly drop, but with near-zero market saturation of NFC-enabled devices, nearly every penny would be wasted, at least in the U.S. market, and at least today.

The Future of NFC: In the future, it can be expected that products ordered will have NFC-embedding as a potential option, whether for posters, various materials, or even coffee mugs, which would potentially take the form of a simple additional text field (like monogramming or personalization), which would then be coded into the materials at the time of production, or even coded after installation. Still, printed technologies like the QR Code will always be more efficient and cost-effective than the addition of the NFC touch-point hardware.

Future applications include nearly everywhere that QR Codes and similar technologies are in use now, but with a built-in, always-on NFC radio, a user could have a very natural, organic interaction with the technologies, by simply waving their phone (or Smart Watch[3], smart ring, etc) at an NFC Touch Point, or perhaps even hear an alarm or notification when a Touch Point is detected. This precludes a difficulty inherent with all QR Code-type technologies: A potential user not knowing what the code is or how to interact with it.

As support for NFC technology grows, we will certainly see a proliferation of applications exploiting the phone's ability to scan the RFID tags, including all of those types mentioned above.

---

[1] *The right-most Tag pictured in black & white is of course on a white background, so the white dots are not visible. They are, of course essential to scanning.*

[2] *Note that I'm not critical of the shortening part here, just the mandatory shortening. Shortening has its place; to reduce data load for high-data content QR Codes by removing the bulk of the data from the matrix. But it's always preferred to keep the data load low and encode the destination URL directly in the matrix.*

---

[3] *Not merely my nod to science fiction. I was introduced to the Pebble brand of smart watches, which link via Bluetooth to Smart Phone apps. Smart "wearables" are appearing all over, so watch for the smart watch that enables or disables technology based on your own hardware tokens, like a smart ring for example. Perhaps on the horizon there would be firearms that could only be fired by a particular person, in the manner of Judge Dredd.*

21. The Future of QR

QR Codes had seen a meteoric rise in popularity throughout the world, most particularly in North America, even as of the 2013 publication of the first edition of this book. As I mentioned in the introduction, some of this is because of the QR Code's obvious utility, on which you should by now be an expert; but clearly, some stems simply from the fact that the QR Code has been '*blessed from on high*': people just like it, for some strange reason, even before we've seen widespread implementation of pretty, useful, or relevant QR Codes and content. They're scanning in droves. Eating it up. It's a mystery.

On some level, I don't feel terribly bold in asserting that this is in significant part because the QR Code has eyes. It looks like a face. Plain and simple. Psychologically, it calls to us: just as infants recognize their mother's face purely on instinct, little chicks in laboratory experiments scurry for cover at the sight of a simulated eagle shadow; some image patterns are attractive and pleasing. Others cause anxiety or revulsion. Much has been made of the objective pattern of facial features associated with subjective beauty. The QR Code is subtly and abstractly evocative of a human face. Thus, we are attracted to it. It isn't quite completely mechanical, and isn't quite entirely foreign.

As direct mail leader Pitney Bowes puts it, QR Codes are *only in their infancy*. Of course, the advance of technology is incessant. Even today, the next generation of print-to-digital linking is developing, and even the sneak-peaks offer astonishing potential, elevating print-to-digital to the level of life-to-digital linking.

Image Recognition and Visual Search

This is implemented already via the Amazon mobile app for smart phones. Snap a photo of an item, and you are magically redirected to the Amazon item purchase page for that item. See something, want something, buy something. You don't even need to know what it is. Just snap any widget you see with a camera, and buy instantly. Of course, when applied more broadly, there are the same issues as with the above QR Code competitors:

A search that begins with a snap of a photo will be impossible for mobile devices to process entirely internally for the foreseeable future. That is, mobile devices will pass the photos to servers with extensive databases, which handle the processing of the image data, then identify the item, and finally redirect the user's browser.

Where will the final destination for the scan be? Google search? eBay item listing? Amazon item? Who will decide where your search ends up? If you have ever used Google search, you know the answer. Your search ends up where Google decides, based on secret algorithms that rank sites (and give favored positioning to sites that pay Google to show their sites first. For a primer on this process, visit

adwords.google.com, where advertisers bid on words to have them appear in your search results.

In the Amazon app example, you know that Amazon is where the purchase will be made, and where you'll be shown matching products. Other attempts to develop this technology are not quite so transparent.

The answer is, the final destination will be wherever the application designer (and their database) decides. Ultimately, this will be determined by whomever will best harmonize the need to creatively monetize your visit for the parties in control of the databases, while crafting a useful User Experience.

Augmented Reality (AR)

The dream of Augmented Reality is the stuff of science fiction: an information overlay to your vision. Simply gaze through your smart phone's camera, and information about objects you see are instantly overlaid in the viewfinder. To see this done well is very impressive. To be sure, these technologies are coming, and they are the future. But, the major question is the form in which they arrive. They are hampered by the same limitations as the above options:

- *There is logically no way to guarantee that objects in the camera will be correctly identified and the desired information displayed.*
- *Tremendous processing overhead assures that large databases are required to process and recognize the images.*
- *This makes the ultimate response of the application subject to the aims and motivations of the database or application developer.*

Google Glass

The ultimate science-fiction implementation of augmented reality that we are promised includes an overlay of web-based information on our everyday environment, as we live. It promises an interactive Heads-Up-Display (HUD), giving directions, recording videos, accessing Social Media accounts and other online information. Alas, they are also near unobtainable due to scarcity, and priced beyond all reason.

WimoReality

Wimo merits additional mention because they are already implementing the future of QR Code technology, today, in the most basic way. The ability to scan logos & images, as well as their own proprietary Triggers, sets them apart in the market. The addition of QR Codes (rather than outright competition with them) would help their product immensely in gaining a better foothold in the market, as Microsoft has done with its *Tag*. Ultimately, only mobile marketing gurus will have nine QR Code scanning apps on their smart phone at any given time, recognize which code they are seeing, and use the right one.

For all other users, the application developers need to be more flexible. Refusing to support the dominant technology in the market is suicide, and does paying clients expecting a payoff from their investment a terrible injustice.

When *anything* can possibly be a hotlink-enabled tag, Best Practices become all the more essential. Identifying what is scannable, and clearly communicating it to consumers is vital. The philosophy I read from these image-recognition tag vendors seems to be that they are trusting consumers to use extra-sensory perception or psychically divine which brands and logos are scannable. That's nonsense. Read my lips: CALL TO ACTION. If communicating what the marking is, what it does, and how to scan it is absolutely indispensible for the dominant technology that most people recognize, it is doubly and triply required for obscure technologies of which the public is entirely ignorant.

Of the few applications I've encountered of the Wimo Reality tags (I've seen only one in the wild), there was no hint provided of what it was or how to use it. And that's not really fair to Wimo… since their white papers are good as well. But their clients just. won't. listen.

Shame, shame.

22. Best Practices

QR Codes (and related, even competing technologies) have a massive potential for allowing anyone to link printed material to their marketing efforts for business, hobby, industry, or nearly any purpose. This potential is tragically untapped, for the most part, due to widespread misunderstanding of precisely how to leverage QR Codes as a coherent response tool as part of Mobile Marketing campaigns. The print & stick paradigm seems to apply as the general rule in QR Code applications, and so by and large, failed or at least underperforming, lackluster implementations are the prevailing norm.

Like many of the things that businesses feel they "just have to have because everyone else has one," they are done poorly, quickly and without the requisite planning.

Thus, information available and readily accessible seems overwhelmingly negative. This is unfortunate, since QR Codes have the unique potential to bring game-changing functionality and facilitate automated and data-rich interactions beyond imagination; certainly beyond the capabilities of any other method.

Microsoft, WimoReality, and other publishers of proprietary QR Code-type technologies go to great lengths to promulgate and publicize tips & tricks, as well as establish *Best Practices* for implementing their tools, including white papers, case studies, and assorted instructional materials to educate consumers, and most especially marketers, to use them intelligently and productively. They even make outright rules that their users are required, by licensing contract, to obey… but don't.

The QR Code field suffers from a lack of coherence and guidance, and essentially no central authority to act as a clearinghouse of sorts to provide guidance, direction and information. It's been a random, chaotic free-for-all, with rank amateurs and ham-fisted bumpkins muddying the waters. But, many of the same rules apply, and strategies applicable to other technologies are, by and large, equally applicable. Thus, it is of primary importance that those active on the QR Code field actively accept and advocate for the greatest possible understanding of the same.

I know what you're thinking: What? Why should I advocate for proper QR Code use? How about I just rock it, and leave those turkeys in my dust!

Good point. Keep in mind that those *turkeys* have you massively outnumbered; if you're trying to do the job right, you're in a tiny minority. And for every customer who scans one of your fabulously well-executed QR Code implementations, ten more are scanning poor implementations that don't work, work poorly, or don't make sense, and are going to be disenchanted with the technology before they ever get to your QR Code. Take a moment to educate your prospects now, and everyone benefits.

Don't worry: The turkeys will never learn, and never progress.

The following is my exhaustive list of QR Code Implementation Best Practices, recommended for every implementation, as applicable, for best results. Most of these ideas are trumpeted by professionals across the entire marketing industry, from top firms and brands, to marketing bloggers and spectators. Ignoring these Best Practices will get your QR Codes ignored, refused, broken, and potentially admitted to the *Hall of Shame Gallery* of the next edition of this book.

1. Trademark Notice

Respect the trademark of the QR Code developers. When using the term "QR Code," be sure to always state, "QR Code is a registered trademark of DENSO WAVE INCORPORATED." It's not merely a recommended Best Practice, but it is also a legal requirement for compliance with their trademarked term. Beyond that, DENSO WAVE created it, so show a little respect. Give them their propers. Nearly any location has room for a few extra words, particularly any magazine or publication that can make a one-time disclosure to cover all advertisers and articles. Ask a publication to work the verbiage into its existing disclaimer block, and give DENSO their propers, as well as bringing every advertiser in the book into compliance. I'd be ticked if someone ripped off this book. If you say "QR Code", mention DENSO.

2. Proper Code Placement

Place QR Codes for maximum impact and scannability. Avoid unsafe, unlikely, and impossible scan locations, including vehicles, billboards, the bottoms of swimming pools (that one trended briefly on social media), or locations from which your prospective QR Code scanning consumer will likely be too distant to successfully scan, in motion when they see it, or otherwise handicapped. Further, avoid online use of QR Codes, whenever possible, *except on pages that are likely to be printed by site visitors*; more can be accomplished with a simple descriptive text hyperlink or even better, an image link. This won't require the user to change from their preferred device, just to scan your QR Code. Why would they do that anyway?

Further, due to differences in screen resolution, scan & refresh rates, QR Codes will always be more difficult to scan from a screen, and so must be larger and take up more space. This is also unpredictable and performance will vary based on type of screen, mobile device, specific scanning application, lighting and many other factors completely beyond your control. QR Codes are for getting to a website, not navigating one. And on a mobile website? Don't even think about it.

The same applies to television. The campaign that Philip Warbasse described during my interview had substantial, multi-million-dollar build-up, and separate marketing campaigns to promote the marketing campaign and get everyone ready to scan… when the code would be displayed for a few seconds during astonishingly-expensive television time, usually valued at six-figures per minute. Unless you have the budget and marketing chops of HBO, please reconsider.

3. A Plain, Text-Only URL

This must always be listed for Non-Scanning Consumers: Allow for consumers to respond by their choice of method. QR Code scanning is popular with Smart Phone users and young people, who are broadly called early adopters of technology. Most other demographics are late adopters and may be completely ignorant of what it is. Include a plain text URL to be typed by those wishing to respond, but unable or unwilling to scan. This further has the benefit of allowing authentication of sorts, so that your consumer can confirm that your QR Code resolves to the correct site visually, by comparing them. Subdomains are best. Direct page navigation, or short URL keywords are also acceptable. Make it easy to type and avoid random or odd characters as well as upper-case. But, do include a tiny variation, such as a query string like "?qr" at the end of the URL, so that scanners and typers can be distinguished.

To not include a text-only URL for non-scanners is to effectively hamstring your campaign and turn it into a dry run experiment demonstrating how many potential customers you lose by marketing only to techie geeks and marketing pros. And, in case of calamity… QR Codes that fail, it provides a backup to disaster. A QR Code without a backup human-readable URL is just plain stupid.

4. Explanation of the Code's Presence.

Get the free mobile app at
http://gettag.mobi

Tell your consumers in brief, straightforward and meaningful terms what the QR Code pattern they're seeing is, how it works, and what content is on the other side, insofar as possible, given space and design considerations for its intended location. Take the time to educate, and help today's late adopters become tomorrow's obsessive scanners. Some of this falls under the umbrella of the call to action, but there's a distinct difference: The call to action is the universal marketing WHAT to do. An explanation of the code's presence is for those who are totally clueless as to what it is, to orient them to WHAT they're seeing.

Consumers have been ignoring barcodes on mail items, consumer product packaging, mailing labels, etc, for decades. If you want them to ignore decades of conditioning, notice a new barcode and actually do something with it, you've gotta clue them in. It's common sense.

Or fail miserably. You decide.

5. A Great Call to Action

Plainly (and politely), invite your consumers to scan your QR Code directly. Tell them, *"Use your Smart Phone and QR Code app to scan here for…"* The Call to Action is a universal marketing concept, and it is a known fact that if you want your target audience demographic to respond, you need to tell them clearly what you want them to do. There's nothing more counterproductive than having ready, willing, able bodies, staring blankly at your marketing message and squandering the opportunity to task them. If you don't tell your marketing prospects what you want them to do, how on earth are they going to do it? Tell them what to do and how to do it.

6. Recommended App Download

Where possible, space permitting of course, recommend the download of a safe, reliable scanning app, and let them know where to get it. Like the QR Codes generated above, which are output all in one piece by Microsoft's Tag generator and Unitag Live's, respectively. A fast, reliable application without useless adware, delays, or proprietary garbage will enhance the QR Code scanning experience and ensure that those who scan today won't be disappointed with the experience and abandon the technology.

I recommend I-Nigma, as stated elsewhere herein, and modify my calls to action to recommend their app, which is excellent and widely available for nearly every Smart Phone OS, and at least the *Big Four.* In this aspect, Microsoft & Unitag's documentation and generator are worlds ahead of other QR Code generators, already offering code downloads such as this one that show the user what to do and direct them to an application to help them do it.

7. Image Quality

Know your medium. On screen, there's no reason for QR Codes higher quality than 70dpi, since screens won't display them higher than that, and a larger file size is just wasted. When intended for printing, keep QR Code images at 300dpi (dots per inch) or higher, as most printing will be this resolution. That seems to be the magic number where the human eye can no longer distinguish pixels in most cases. Below this resolution, or using 70dpi (computer screen resolution) QR Code images will present a grainy, low-resolution image that looks unprofessional and sloppy, or isn't distinct enough to scan reliably. Obtain original .png, .pdf, or .jpg files and archive them for use. Don't photocopy an old QR Code or degrade their appearance. Re-generate them if need be, it isn't hard.

Be wary of print methods: home inkjet and any laser printer will work great, but commercial inkjets on glossy paper printed at high speeds may compromise print quality.

8. Display Size

Space is always at a premium on any marketing piece, from a business card to a billboard. As they say, *real estate is the one thing they're not making more of.* No matter what your medium is, that's all the space you have. And it's never enough to say everything you want to say. But, always allow functional elements the space they need. Don't make them too small, or they'll be too discrete to notice (or too tiny to scan), and don't make them too large, either; They aren't high art or mere decoration, they are functional; use them as they are intended. The absolute size of a QR Code is largely determined by the resolution of the camera of the mobile device that scans it. But, assuming a low-resolution, low-data QR Code, stick with ¾-1 inch for most uses. Many cameras simply can't focus closer than 4-5 inches (or with a resolution to make up for the distance), and scans at that range will be difficult. In its Tag Implementation Guide, Microsoft defines the ratio of code size to scan distance as 1 to 7.5, which I think is a great place to draw the line. So, stick to the rule of 7: keep the QR Code no smaller than 1/7th of the anticipated scan distance. This means, if a distance of 7 inches is most likely (for, example, a direct mail piece held in one's hand), make the QR Code at least ¾-1 inch wide. Similarly, if a QR Code appears on a billboard from which viewers (and scanners) will likely be 150 feet away, be sure that your QR Code is around 22 feet tall. Sound absurd? I agree. Why do you think billboard QR Codes get such a bad rap in the preceding chapters? Because a typical billboard is no taller than 14'.

9. Error Correction

Use a generator that allows you to select the Error correction level. Error correction adds redundant, duplicate data, and increases the data load (and thus, the pattern density & complexity). So, use good judgment in choosing an error correction level. For online display, where damage simply isn't possible, use Low error correction… it's useless in this case. For disposable items that will be digitally printed clearly, use Low or Medium error correction to save space. For long-term campaigns or on objects that might be subject to wear & tear and need to last, or when printing using a low-resolution printing method, like on fabric, or a rubber stamp, or when you plan to artistically alter a QR Code to create a designer code, use Quality or High error correction. More isn't always better. Overkill is just inefficiency.

And remember: error correction won't help if the whole QR Code is printed blurry. In that case, you'd be better off with the slightly simpler QR Code with low error correction.

10. Follow the Ground Rules

Keep a solid Quiet Zone around your QR Code; less is often just fine, but don't butt your code against other elements, for best scanning as well as neatest appearance. Don't tamper with or obscure the Finder Pattern or Orientation Pattern, or other key features, being especially careful when deliberately altering a QR Code by hand to create a Designer QR Code. When editing by hand, or dressing-up a QR Code, be judicious, and don't get greedy. Just a touch of color is all that's needed. A small logo is a lovely touch. Better to impress with your company's color scheme, and a small logo than risk the QR Code not scanning at all. In any case, test, test, test.

11. Direct URL Access

When possible and technically feasible, code the ultimate Landing Page destination directly into the QR Code, so that the scanning app can resolve it instantly and display the destination web page quickly.

The best way to do this is to use a short subdomain of your website, which promotes consistency, branding, simplicity and reliability. A short "slug" for Direct Page navigation is another way to use Direct Access URLs, as is a CMS Query String. But note that this does take some slight technical chops. Often it's more practical, though potentially less reliable to just shorten the URL:

12. URL Shortening

When needed, if Direct Access, Friendly Hosting, and/or Reducing Data Density is just not feasible for you, use a URL Shortener to cut the character length of the URL (or any information) coded into the QR Code. This makes for a neat, uniform appearance for QR Codes, quick recognition by scanning apps, more reliable printing for all print methods, with just a small, usually imperceptible delay resolving to the destination URL.

Use URL shortening judiciously and only when necessary, as it will add Latency – millisecond-length delays in resolving to the desired website – and can introduce Fail Points – additional complexity that can go wrong and leave a user stranded, thus ruining the user experience. URL Shortening can allow you to use infinite tricks, but if your use isn't very ambitious, Direct URL Access is better (for example, adding Google custom campaign link tracking tags to them, or coding in a customer's ID number, etc).

13. Offer Friendly URLs

Whether this means a Landing Page on your own site with a short URL, using a sub-domain or subdomains on your own site, a URL Shortening service, setting up the *vanity* Your Own URL Shortener on your site, or simply opting for a more reputable and recognizable shortener, do it. The subdomain is recommended, as it can incorporate multiple Best Practices, being direct, friendly, re-directable and with a little know-how, trackable. YOURLS can be hosted on your domain, and is great for this. Bit.ly can also integrate with your site at the Domain Name Service level to give you their full functionality on your own domain.

Whatever method you choose, know this: A smart consumer is wary not to just click any link or scan any code. If your QR Code or the link it represents is just alphanumeric gibberish, it doesn't build trust. Your customers know your name and know what they expect from you, so give it to them and reinforce the good will and brand identity you've already built. It wasn't free. It was very expensive. Use it!

14. Redirectable URL

The ability to change the destination URL of a short URL can be a life-saver, money-saver, campaign-saver, business-saver, and job-saver. Everyone makes mistakes; nobody's perfect. Being able to swap out the destination URL is just good business, whether to make a fancy Designer QR Code re-usable, to pull your fat out of the fire when you make a terrible mistake, or when Murphy's Law applies… or the completely unexpected arises. Coding a subdomain of your website into the QR Code is ideal for all purposes, and satisfies every option, as you may specify that your subdomain land anywhere. Alternately, any URL Shortener can be used, as long as URLs can be redirected. For this purpose, YOURLS is in, QRStuff is in, Bit.ly is out.

15. Low Data Density

Keep the data encoded in your QR Codes short and sweet. A "Version 2" QR Code (21x21 pixel matrix) is distinct, clear, and scans readily and easily, holding up to ~30 characters, more than enough for most URLs. Don't get greedy for data. Beyond Version 3 (see QR Code data in URL Shortening chapter), shorten the URL or use a clever subdomain redirection, or you risk scan failures, poor user experience, and annoyed consumers. Remember, the more data stored, the slower and less reliably the scanning application will recognize and resolve it, and the more failure prone things get. So, use one of the above methods to keep your data load as low as you can, and if that's just not possible, Shorten the URL: it's an OK solution, every time, even if not "technically" the top choice.

16. Be Secure

Secure your site. Don't be hacked or have your Landing Pages disappear right out from under you. Don't subject your visitors, customers, and QR Code-scanning consumers to potential fraud or abuse. Get an SSL certificate, and tell your customers all about it. Advertise your secure checkout and look good. Customize your QR Codes to make them harder to fake or replace. Use alternate text so scanners know where they're going.

17. Track & Analyze

Don't let your efforts go to waste. You work hard for your business and need every bit of your work… working for you. You want your customers to respond, and get in contact with you, and when they do, it's great. But, don't miss the opportunity to make your campaign trackable. Whether you just count click-throughs using a URL shortener, send visitors to a Formstack or Wufoo webform or landing page and trust them with your analytics, or formal, integrated Mobile Website solutions such as UnitagLive, Tappinn and Mofuse, or use advanced analytics or conversion & ROI calculations through Google Analytics, there's a workable solution for everybody, at every level of technical competence.

Do it. It will give you information on what sort of response you're getting, what you're doing well, and how to do it better next time. Do it, set it up, check to see if it's collecting data, and then forget about it. Even if you know you won't have time to review the reports. Because everybody hits a bump in the road at some point, and wants to know *why. What the heck happened? No calls? No form submissions? Did ANYONE even look this way?* When that time comes, if you didn't bother setting it up, you'll wish you had.

Beyond that, and despite my love of QR Codes, it bears mentioning that they're no panacea. Maybe they won't work for you, your medium, your practices, your marketing, your campaigns, your customers, clients, prospects, and leads. If not, dump them. You'll have the data and know for sure.

18. Color & Design

Stand out! Why are all these QR Codes everywhere looking so lame? Anyone can create a gorgeous masterpiece for free, based on a short URL, or a Landing Page dedicated to that QR Code, and then re-use it forever by just changing the short URL destination periodically, or refreshing the Landing Page content. Add security to your QR Codes by making them more difficult to spoof, copy, simulate, or counterfeit. Remember: crooks are lazy. They won't Photoshop an amazing QR Code masterpiece to match yours… they'll harass someone easier.

Enhance your brand recognition with your company colors, logo and info, and build interest and curiosity with your consumers for higher response. And it's easy! There's no reason not to, and every reason to do it, NOW. This QR took 10 minutes to create for free, and could have your logo in another two.

19. Mobilize

You can be assured that every single Landing Page or website visitor who arrives via QR Code scan got there on a Mobile Device, almost guaranteed to be a Smart Phone. These devices have small screens and limited features for navigation, as compared to desktop computers. Anticipate the needs of your visitors and create a positive User Experience for them by making sure that your site is Mobile-friendly, and displays a version of your site (or a different site) that is easy to view and use on their phones. There are so many ways to do this, many of which are easy, and all of which are economical. No excuses. If you don't have a mobile site experience waiting, don't use a QR Code. Your visitors will land on a useless site, full of content they can't see or use, the second-worst possible mobile experience. Use a mobile CMS theme, a Responsive theme or website template, ideally with mobile browser detection and redirects, or just a separate mobile site.

20. Proper Function

The number one, worst-possible mobile experience is the site that doesn't work at all. This refers both to the QR Code itself being functional and legible, as well as the Landing Page working properly. Broken links, missing Landing Pages, mobile site subscription service unpaid but still directing visitors into oblivion, pages not found or generating errors, promised content not present. Nearly half of all QR Codes I find in the wild are dead on arrival, and people blame the QR Code? Do people blame the Internet if I have a non-existent website on my business card? So…

21. Test, Test, Re-Test

And then test Some More: Test when you create a QR Code, with as many varied devices and apps as you can get your hands on. At least test with one of each, iOS, Android, Blackberry & Windows phones, even if you have to beg passersby to scan it, or hang out in the Wal-Mart electronics section borrowing their display phones. Test again when you create your marketing material. Test again immediately before launch, just to be sure. And test periodically during the campaign, so that if your Landing Pages go down, or anything goes wrong, you'll be the first to know… and take corrective action.

22. Content is King

Consumers need a reason to visit. Make it interesting, make it entertaining, make it useful, make it relevant to the visitor, and then make it known (see Call to Action, above), or they won't visit. And most importantly, keep your promises; don't advertise special offers and content, only to have your consumers arrive on your page to discover that it's all missing. What a let-down! The QR Code and your C2A may get people there, but those are just numbers on a report, not dollars in your pocket, if they don't engage, contact you, and purchase product or service. The landing is your moment to shine… don't choke.

23. Professional QR Code Validation

It's not appropriate for every situation… I've launched $300 campaigns for as many clients as I've launched $30,000 campaigns, and obviously you can't spend the whole budget, art, paper, postage and all, just to prove a QR Code works on all 2,403 devices on the market.

But, if you're in this campaign for 6-figures (or whatever is beyond your comfort level to the extent that it hinges on the QR Code to hold things together) and the QR Code response is vital in the situation, pay a testing service to troubleshoot with an army of phones. It can cost under $500. Spring for custom QR Code validation services, that test your QR Code's validity and function with dozens of platforms and Mobile Device Operating systems, so that reliability will never be a question. This is really only necessary when a QR Code has been artistically compromised and a campaign is expensive enough to warrant the extra steps needed to ensure perfect function… like a multi-million-dollar coordinated product.

24. Make it Social: Have Social Media buttons or links, to allow your visitors to share their experience with others, or (and this can be trickier), create automated Social Media interactions based on their visit, or activities. Form submissions can be translated into Tweets or posts, and contests or offers can be extended to everyone. Incentivize sharing and make it viral.

25. Privacy

Although I've made note of a number of strategies for tracking response to individual QR Code scanners, keep in mind that it's best to preserve your customer's privacy and not unnecessarily send private, personal information over the internet. There is certainly the potential to take the strategies I've described herein too far.

Take the full name, address, etc, example that I've shown in the advanced strategy chapter. That's an impressive demo that shows what's possible. It's not for direct imitation. The way this is actually done is by sending an anonymous token, which is discretely matched to the customer or prospect's information in your database, by server-side functions on your web server. So, the individual's actual information never actually gets sent.

Keep in mind that there are pieces of information that are governed by special legislation, to include credit (Fair Credit Reporting Act), mortgage, housing (Equal Housing Opportunity), government, education & medical data (Healthcare Information Privacy & Portability Act), just to name a few. Before testing the limits of this technology, be sure that you're aware of the ramifications of these issues for your industry. Many nations and local governments are taking action to protect their citizens' privacy on line, so this field is certainly in flux, and staying abreast of ongoing developments is essential. Beyond specific legal issues, sending your customers' data across the internet is generally a bad idea. Google and other companies prohibit the use of data markers that are "personally identifiable," and will immediately make your valuable visitor data disappear if anyone realizes that you are sending personally-identifiable visitor information in your URLs.

26. Organize Your Codes

If you're dabbling in QR Codes, and finding more and more uses for your business, you're going to start accumulating plenty of them. Keeping them organized with a system that archives the images, and allows you to change their colors, destination page or re-generate them is ideal. Once again, I recommend QRStuff.com, whose dashboard allows filing, grouping, re-naming, re-coloring, re-directing, and nearly any other function to manage your codes. YOURLS also has some of the same functions, when outfitted with QR Code generator plugin,

23. Chapter 20: Conclusion

We have come to the end of our journey together, and now you'll need to begin your own journey. I wish you success and excellence in your future endeavors, in all areas, but most specifically in marketing and applying QR Codes to your business needs.

I sincerely hope that you'll take some time to visit, share your thoughts on this book, perhaps write a review, browse some of the additional, amplified content, download a tool or two, perhaps ask a question, upload a QR Code of your own creation, or share a case study of your own crowning successes or humiliating failures in marketing with QR Codes (I once saw one get inverted through a simple flick of the wrist while using Photoshop; they don't scan in the mirror). I sincerely hope you choose to take advantage.

By all means, if this book made good on its promises, please visit one of the following pages where the book is sold, and take the time to review it. More than likely, you purchased at least one or two books or eBooks on this subject before arriving at this one, and so you're the best authority on what's out there.

I know that I wasn't able to find anything like this in my research for this book, and all these lessons came the hard way… through the school of hard knocks. If you've benefitted from these concepts, please take the time to review the book. Scan here, or type our short URL to visit:

http://eshlepper.com/review

24. Glossary of Terms

Adwords: Google's advertising program, in which advertisers can bid on keyword combinations, and set a price for having their advertisements appear in Google search results.

API: Application Programmer Interface. A language (more or less standardized) for interacting with web services using online scripts and programs (rather than visiting the site yourself).

Augmented Reality (AR): The future of QR Code technology: instead of your Smart Phone's camera scanning a barcode-style link and using it's browser to access content, objects are recognized through image recognition, and data is overlaid in on your phone's screen, much like a "heads-up display." Truly, this is the stuff of science fiction. There are many great applications out there, but the walk-around-and-see-cool-stuff-overlaid-everywhere-like-sci-fi-goggles applications that we have been promised are several generations away. First we have to move through the development spectrum past NFC.

Best Practices: Acknowledged and recommended standard policies in an industry that dictate the most effective, responsible, and appropriate methods for accomplishing a task. Best practices may refer to the most useful techniques, but can also refer to a combination of techniques that leads the way for future regulatory changes or ensures the best possible legal compliance. Herein, usually the former is intended, unless specified otherwise.

The "Big Four": The four top-selling, top-scanning, highly-supported Smart Phone operating systems, iOS (iPhone, iPad & iPod), Android OS, Windows Mobile and Blackberry/RIM (Research In Motion). Although, to be fair, Blackberry is really an insignificant part of scanning volume, but it's at least present.

BlotCode: Unique, inkblot-shaped proprietary QR Code. Visually interesting (I personally find it the second most attractive of all, but extremely limited technically, and virtually unsupported by major Smart Phone manufacturers & app developers. No one at all seems to be using it. Perhaps this is what happens when someone launches a proprietary technology without the backing & clout of a company the size of Microsoft. See the chapter on "QR Code Competitors" for details.

Brand Advertising: Mass-market advertising focusing entirely on a single brand. Brand advertising is distinct from Direct Response Advertising in that it is designed to generally increase awareness and curiosity about a brand, but is not necessarily aimed at generating actual product purchases, but rather at building awareness, reputation, and name-recognition of a brand, its logos, logotypes, and trademarks. This is most useful for very large, established and nationally- or globally-recognizable brands that do business exclusively through distributors: they don't care which distributor you visit to purchase your Coca-Cola, for example. Lack of useful contact information in an advertisement or a specific call to action is a hallmark of brand advertising… since it doesn't matter to the ad creator where the item is purchased.

Campaign: A single marketing effort, characterized by basic stated goals, methods, and time frame.

Data Matrix: Technically, data matrix is the only technology able to compete (or even compare) with QR Codes directly, and has similarly massive data-storage capabilities and features, even exceeding those of the the QR Code by a small margin. Why has data matrix not been blessed with popularity and been relegated to industrial applications? Anyone's guess. Discussion of Data Matrix codes has been omitted from the chapter on "QR Code Competitors" because they are not in use in marketing.

Denso Wave Incorporated: Toyota subsidiary that holds (though it doesn't enforce) the patent on the coding scheme for QR Codes, as well as the trademark for the words "QR Code" (which it does enforce). QR Code is a trademark of DENSO WAVE INCORPORATED. See? Be sure to use this tagline anywhere you make reference to a "QR Code."

Designer QR Code: An artistic masterpiece of a QR Code, incorporating color, rounded edges, patterns, gradients, logos, or other elements, usually hand-edited in photo editing software, and one of a kind. Often the break the ground rules of what is recommended for a QR Code to scan properly, stretching the limits of the Quiet Zone, Orientation Marks, etc. This can be done to impressive effect, but requires care so that codes still scan properly.

Dotcode: Yet another technology similar to QR Codes, which is also proprietary and used almost exclusively for parcel tracking purposes. United Parcel Service (UPS) uses dotcodes to track their parcels. Omitted from discussion in the "QR Code Competitors" chapter because they simply aren't in use for marketing purposes.

Direct Access/Indirect Access: This refers to how a user is directed to the Landing Page for a QR Code. Direct Access means coding the full URL to the intended Landing Page into the QR Code. This yields the benefits of simplicity, speed & reliability for the visitor, but can be more technically demanding to set up. Indirect Access, on the other hand, means shortening the URL destination of a QR Code; this, in turn requires an intermediate step of visiting the URL shortener site, and then re-directing to the final destination. This can add a few seconds to the process, and make it less transparent to the visitor, but offers a number of benefits for the non-professional on a budget.

Direct Mail: Sending items using postage, via the United States Postal Service, ie, the snail mail. Which shouldn't be taken as pejorative, merely as a reality of mail; it is slower than Email. Direct Mail is, and for the foreseeable future will continue to be one of the most potent channels for marketing, though it is often neglected in favor of online marketing, Email or Social Media marketing, by virtue of their perceived low entry cost. In truth, to do any of these right and productively, substantial expense, time, and know-how may be involved.

Direct Response Marketing: In contrast with Brand Advertising, Direct Response (DR) Marketing or Advertising is specifically intended to produce a customer response and contact via one or more means, and result in a sale of a product or service within a specific time frame. Special offers, limited-time pricing, contests, coupons, or offer codes are hallmarks of Direct Response Marketing, and are all ways of quantifying and discriminating sales generated by, and attributable to, a given campaign.

DIY (Do-It-Yourself): The bootstrapping, bare-bones, on-the-cheap way of doing things: all by your lonesome. My favorite way. Unfortunately for most, it also usually requires that you stop what you're doing, whether it's making money, running a business, servicing customers, and generating new leads, to stop dead and try to learn some trivial arcane information or skills (like web programming, response tracking, etc). It's the point of this book, but can be a very difficult proposition. Unfortunately, without large amounts of investment capital or a specific budget for outsourcing, it can be the only possible way to do things for many businesses.

Dynamic/Variable QR Codes: These are often confused terms. No QR Code is truly "Variable," as each individual coded image is fixed. However, these terms are commonly used (confusingly, and interchangeably to refer to two different things): First, "Dynamic" QR Codes are those that use a referrer or URL shortener, and thus, their Landing Page can be changed without the need to re-generate a QR Code. This enables re-use of artistic QR Codes, as well as allowing for the Landing Page to be corrected if errors were made in coding it, or if it was redirected. Obviously, everyone plans for everything to always be perfect, 100% of the time. However, when Mr. Murphy comes a'callin', it's nice to be able to easily fix it, especially with thousands of QR Codes printed already… which is why it's a Best Practice. The term Variable QR Codes is also used to refer to a series of QR Codes pre-generated, or generated on-the-fly, that are each unique (for example, for all the recipients of a post-card, or each visitor to a website); however, this is a misnomer, as each individual code is a fixed, unique code – there is no variance to speak of.

Email Marketing: "Eblasts" are an organized, focused, and purpose-driven campaign intended to contact customers via email and gauge their response. This is distinct from simply emailing customers with a special. Email marketing, when done well, uses trackable links to gauge interest, even when no actual response or purchase results. This helps fine-tune future marketing efforts and identify potentially interested customers, who can received improved marketing emails, or even more expensive direct mail, phone calls, or other marketing media. When done poorly, it can be ineffective, harassing, and even illegal. Some recommended solutions for small businesses include Constant Contact (www.constantcontact.com), and Mail Chimp, (www.mailchimp.com).

Formstack: Formstack.com One of the premier web-form hosting services on the internet. Makes it easy to create and manage all your forms in one place, modify them with a WYSIWYG interface, and update them all together without the need to edit the individual sites where they are hosted directly. Formstack's user experience is quite similar to other services, and well-suited to the novice, with zero knowledge of web development. There is only a limited trial account for free, but the paid service price compares favorably to Formstack. More complicated things are possible with Formstack, and it is in fact my own form hosting solution of choice. Designed to integrate with a host of services, too lengthy to list, but including eMail Marketing services (such as Constant Contact), or even item purchases with Paypal. See also Wufoo.

Friendly URL Hosting: Hosting your own content, to build credibility, trust, and the appearance of safety & security. An example would be using a mobile-optimized Landing Page with your YouTube video embedded, rather than simply linking to the video in YouTube. Thus, your link would be www.MySite.com/coolvideo, or coolvideo.mysite.com rather than www.youtube.com/lk2RgkQc, or a shortened URL such as bit.ly/k2rgQclP. The latter seems contrived and unprofessional. The former builds your brand, makes the link "sticky" by not funneling visitors off (or circumventing) your site, where they'll get lost browsing videos of cats doing silly things and dogs dancing.

Google Analytics: The standard in online traffic tracking. "GA", as it is frequently abbreviated, involves the set-up of an account to track your websites, and a short script code that is added to each page that will be tracked. When a visitor lands on a web page with the Google Analytics tracking code, the script is activated, the page visit is counted, and various browser & demographic information about the visitor is recorded, which can later be reviewed through the online dashboard.

Kinetic Roadside Advertising: Trend in recent years, of road-size sign-men (often in costumes or flambuoyant clothing), dancing, shaking, tossing, waving, and generally making a high-energy (kinetic) spectacle with their signs to attract attention from drivers.

Landing Page: Your visitor's point of arrival at your website. This may or may not even be on your site, but may be a separate mobile-optimized version of your site, a web form, Blog, video, or check-out page hosted elsewhere. Landing pages are useful as they are customized to the current campaign with appropriate text and offers, heavily mobile optimized (as their only visitors will be mobile users, assuming arrival through a QR Code scan), and they are (or should be) trackable, as they are the unique point of entry, so unlike home pages, all traffic generated is known to be from the current specific campaign for which it was created.

Lifestyle Advertising: Advertising aimed at selling an image or idea of a user of a product. Examples include popular advertising campaigns for sporting or luxury goods. Campaigns focus on the character of customers or the portrayal of the high-level of customers' quality of life, often in intangible or purely inspirational ways unrelated to the product itself.

Managed Solutions: Managed means just what it sounds like: the marketing channel is managed by a marketing company, including setting up the campaign, Landing Pages, hosting media, tracking response, etc. Managed solutions are guaranteed to be the slickest, most productive, impressive, and easiest. They are also going to be the most expensive, as the significant technical expertise required can often have a steep price tag, although usually there are varied price points. If you're not marketing a national brand with a near-unlimited budget, See DIY, or turn to page 1 and let's get started.

Microsoft Tag: Microsoft's entry into the proprietary QR Code realm. Numerous benefits, notably that it is designed to work along with QR Codes, and not to entirely compete against them. Also, their interface allows a number of excellent options. See the chapter on "QR Code Competitors" for details.

Mobile Marketing: Marketing with a focus on the wireless device (phone & Smart Phone) users & their unique needs, desires, experiences, and preferred methods of interacting. This can include mobile-optimized websites, code-scan techniques such as QR Codes & the other similar technologies detailed herein, the emerging NFC technology, web forms that capture location data from Smart Phone operating systems, SMS and SMS Short-Code interactions, and other techniques of engaging and interacting with the consumer via their mobile devices.

Mobile (Optimized) Website: A website designed specifically to be compatible with or to be gracefully displayed on the smaller screens of Smart Phones and other mobile devices, providing a user experience for them. Features include small size (or at least narrow & tall), larger buttons to exploit touch-screens, rather than small hypertext links, scrolling select menus, etc, that are easy to use on Smart Phones. Conversely, features that would be difficult to use or view are eliminated.

Mobile Tagging: Use of QR Codes and similar technologies for quick response via Smart Phone scan.

Mobile Visual Search (MVS): A similar emerging technology. Much like Augmented Reality (AR), image recognition of the objects or images themselves trigger searches or find items photographed, either displaying information about the item, or online store listings to purchase the item, etc (emphasis on the latter). As with most conceivable AR technologies, ultimately the destination or information overlaid is controlled by the app developer or the database used to identify the objects. Whether these technologies work well for the user will depend on how the companies controlling the technology decide to monetize it. If everything you scan leads you to my own online storefront (or Amazon's), the technology is limited.

NFC: Near-Field Communication. A radio-transponder based technology akin to RFID (Radio Frequency Identification) tags, that allow a device to scan the electromagnetic signature of an NFC "touch point" to read data and direct to a URL. Fundamentally different from other technologies discussed herein, as an actual piece of electromagnetic recording media must be embedded in the media, and similarly, the Smartphone's Hardware must be equipped to scan.

Open Technology: The opposite of Proprietary Technology. Open Technologies are not based in secret algorithms and are generally not patented (or, like the QR Code patent, the owner declines to enforce its patent rights), making the technology usable by all. This openness has led to a massive proliferation of QR Codes that dwarfs any other competing technology, to a staggering degree.

Orientation Pattern: The most obvious and notable QR Code feature; the three squares-within-squares at the corners of the QR Code. These are the first features that a scanning application looks for, in order to identify the pattern as a QR Code before decoding it. Tampering excessively with the Orientation Patterns can result in an unscannable QR Code.

Proprietary Technology: Technology that is someone's *property*; the opposite of Open Technology: Technologies are called proprietary when they are the property of a single company or persons who have the legal authority to restrict their use, usually through patent or patent and trademark. Often herein, I decry these technologies, as they can be less accessible, less useful, and less broadly utilized than open technologies (like the QR Code). Generally, proprietary bar codes can only be generated or scanned with their patent holder's generator or scanner app, and all traffic runs through their site first (and is under their control and proceeds only with their blessing). In a nutshell, with proprietary technologies, your codes go where and do what the owner says (not what you say). This isn't entirely different than using a QR Code exclusively with a single URL shortener, except that you could never change services, and would have to throw away the entire technology (and every piece of material with the marks on it, if you did). In other words, you would never own anything that you put the mark on, and would be instantly in violation of the owner's copyright if your relationship with the owner ended. Seems pretty complicated, just to make a little black mark. And that's one of the key reasons why this book is about QR Codes, and not the other technologies.

QR Code: "Quick Response Code" is a 2-Dimensional bar code, conforming to the specifications of ISO 18004, invented by, and a trademark of DENSO WAVE INCORPORATED. See Chapter 1. If you've read this book, and still don't know what a QR Code is, please contact me for a prompt refund.

Quiet Zone: A thin isolation area, or border of light color, preferably white that ensures that scanning applications will be able to discern the QR Code features and data from surrounding art or text on a page. The recommended Quiet Zone is quite large, but can be reduced substantially, and still yield a good, scannable QR Code. But, there are limits.

Responsive Website Design: Websites designed to naturally adjust to the visitor's device, displaying content appropriate for the device used. Mobile sites get single-column, streamlined content; Tablets get wider content. Desktops get full-featured versions. An easy way to mobile optimize quickly and cheaply. Responsive sites will not generally have the simplicity of true mobile sites, but will display acceptably on mobile devices if care is taken in their design.

RFID: Radio Frequency IDentification. Tracking technology that is based on recordable and detectable magnetic fields, stored in tracking tokens. Common uses include theft-prevention tags used in retail stores (sometimes concealed invisibly in products), Speed-Pay-type keyfobs used pay for fuel at gas stations (through a link to a credit card), access badges that are scanned to allow facility access, and pet "micro-chipping" for identification. Near-Field Communication (NFC) is a type of RFID technology, simply re-branded and re-marketed for a new purpose.

Variable/Dynamic QR Codes: These are often confused terms. No QR Code is truly "Variable," as each individual coded image is fixed. However, these terms are commonly used (confusingly, and interchangeably to refer to two different things): First, "Dynamic" QR Codes are those that use a referrer or URL shortener, and thus, their Landing Page can be changed without the need to re-generate a QR Code. This enables re-use of artistic QR Codes, as well as allowing for the Landing Page to be corrected if errors were made in coding it, or if it was redirected. Obviously, everyone plans for everything to always be perfect, 100% of the time. However, when Mr. Murphy comes a'callin', it's nice to be able to easily fix it, especially with thousands of QR Codes printed already… which is why it's a Best Practice. The term Variable QR Codes is also used to refer to a series of QR Codes pre-generated, or generated on-the-fly, that are each unique (for example, for all the recipients of a post-card, or each visitor to a website); however, this is a mis-nomer, as each individual code is a fixed, unique code – there is no variance to speak of.

Sandwich Man: Old-fashioned street signage (the original "kinetic roadside" advertisement). Two signs, joined at the top with a hinge, and worn on a person's front and back side, to show the marketing message in two directions. A stationary sign without a person "sandwiched" in it and carrying it would be a "sandwich board."

ShotCode: Unique, round target-shaped proprietary code scan option. Visually interesting, but extremely limited technically, and virtually unsupported by major Smart Phone manufacturers & app developers. Seems to have a bevy of big-names and major corporations utilizing it, although I have yet to see one in the wild.

Nor have you. See the chapter on "QR Code Competitors" for details.

Slug: Content Management System term referring to a URL-safe version of a website name (ie, not containing any characters that need to be URL encoded, such as spaces). Usually slugs are all lower-case, with hyphens substituted for spaces.

Smart Phone: A modern mobile phone with built-in functions similar to a mobile computer, including email, an internet browser, media players, cameras, and installable applications and programs.

Subdomain: Subdivision of a website domain, generally taking the place of the www.

TLD (Top-Level-Domain): The .com or .org at the end of a URL; managed by a top-level web authority or nation's IT infrastructure. The largest division of the world wide web.

UI (User Interface): Also GUI (Graphical User Interface). The point of interaction with an application or website. These are generally unique to devices, although in the case of websites, the website designer is entirely free to design the UI almost without limits. To say there is a right way and a wrong way would be wrong: But, there are basic features and concepts that have evolved into expected standards for users. Deviation is not recommended.

URL: Universal Resource Locator: a web address. The unique location of a specific file on the internet.

URL Shortener: An online service that provides a short URL (website address, ie, http://www.______________.com) that can be used in lieu of a longer url, to fit into a Tweet, to prevent email clients from breaking lines (and links), or to hide the true destination of a link. Examples include bit.ly and ow.ly, as well as my own eshlepper.com (the use of very short domain names makes it possible to have the shortest shortened URLs possible). In addition to these

UX (User Experience): The unique experience generated by your website or other media when used by your customers, prospects, visitors, etc. The UX is the ultimate determinating factor of how your visitors will respond to your media, whether they choose to accept, reject, leave the site, engage and purchase, share, etc. Much of the user experience centers around making the site or media easy and natural to use, including Mobile Optimization, attractiveness, focus, flow, etc. Can be very subjective, but there are common aspects to good UX.

Validation: The process of verifying that a QR Code scans properly on the broadest range of devices & operating systems, as well as with the broadest range of scanning apps. Certainly always a great idea, but can be pricey, ranging from $100-500. Truly, this is only cost-effective when planning a massive, national campaign, and using a designer code that has had its vital features "artistically compromised". Otherwise, if a QR Code is being used as generated, and on a small scale, rarely is this needed or worth the price.

Viral: The Holy Grail – the ultimate goal in web content advertising; when the entertainment value of content is so engaging that it takes on a life of its own, and online users actively spread it on their own, without any active action on the marketer's part. They simply share it on Social Media, forward it around via an email chain or joke spam, post to Blogs & repost in multiple media, etc, because of the entertainment or interest value of the content itself.

WimoReality Triggers: A unique entry into the proprietary QR Code realm. The uniqueness of this offering is that the user has the ability to use WiMo's unique trigger images, or even allow customers to scan logos and images as one would scan a QR Code. Numerous benefits and drawbacks. Personally, I find Wimo's proprietary trigger images the most attractive and inviting of all QR Code wannabees. See the chapter on "QR Code Competitors" for details.

Wordpress: The Pre-Eminent Website CMS (Content Management System). Commonly associated with the Wordpress.org blogging site, many are not aware that Wordpress.com offers free downloads of the Wordpress system for installation on any hosted web space. Far more than a blogging system, tens of thousands of customizable themes and skins are available to build a full-featured website of nearly any level of complexity, and free and publicly-available plugins can add mobile functionality, ecommerce functions, QR Code generation, Social Media functions, and nearly any functionality imaginable.

Wufoo: www.wufoo.com One of the premier web-form hosting services on the internet. Makes it easy to create and manage all your forms in one place, modify them with a WYSIWYG interface, and update them all together without the need to edit the individual sites where they are hosted directly. Wufoo's user experience is top notch, and well-suited to the novice, with zero knowledge of web development. A free account will host up to three forms (with some limitations on the complexity & functionality), while a paid account will allow complex interactions and responsive forms that can integrate with Social Media, eMail Marketing services (such as Mail Chimp), or even item purchases with Paypal. See also Formstack.

YOURLS: Your **O**wn **URL S**hortener**.** Self-installable, self-hosted so-called *vanity* URL shortener.

WYSIWYG: What-You-See-Is-What-You-Get: An online user experience with a generator that is designed to show the end product as it is created, to allow a novice without programming experience to easily use the site.

25. QR Code Software

Below is a more extensive list of QR Code scanning apps & services than was possible in the previous chapters. Each has it's own charms & issues, as well as limitations & strengths. You're encouraged to explore these and find a solution that's right for you, or refer to previous chapters for information on building your own custom-QR Code generating website with the free downloadable tools suggested there.

It should also be noted that many are going the way of the dodo – with camera phone software now readily identifying and scanning QR Codes natively, the value of dedicated QR Code scanning apps is falling.

So, this list can be viewed as a historical record of many of these.

1. *iNigma – As stated previously, my own favorite scanner. Simply the most reliable and fastest I've used. Highly Recommended.*
2. *NeoReader – Also quite easy to use, but has a terribly difficult time scanning from computer screens due to refresh rates, etc. I like it because it always starts on the home screen, ready to scan. Recommended.*
3. *Scanlife - Good function, but one of the most heavily monetized of apps. Display ads and suggested products make it annoying.*
4. *Red Laser - A good, fast scanner. This was my go-to scanner for quite a long time. Supports 1-D barcode scans as well in some versions & devices. Recommended.*
5. *QR+ - Not a particularly good scanner, but has two highly noteworthy features: First, it allows creation & emailing of QR Codes directly from the mobile device, with a choice of colors as well (and even some embedded text). Second, it is able to process photographs on the mobile device for QR Code images. Very useful.*
6. *Microsoft Tag Scanner – Quality scanner, useful for both Tags & QR Codes. Recommended.*
7. *2D Sense – The only tag scanner that purports to scan Blotcodes, has options for Shotcodes also, and even supports Data Matrix and QR Codes. My own experience places it at the bottom of the list for QR Code scanning. Generally low performance.*
8. *For Best QR Code generation results, go directly to the source. Download DENSO WAVE INCORPORATED's desktop QR Code generation software for free, here: http://www.denso-wave.com/en/adcd/download/category/soft-driver/qr/list.html*
9. *"Zebra Crossing" is an open-source repository of various utilities for processing bar code images, hosted by Google. Some very useful options include the QR Code image*

upload & decode function.
http://code.google.com/p/zxing/

10. *Assorted Links and Resources for Online QR Code Generation (Fancy)*

http://www.print2d.com - Print2D is the site of Philip Warbasse of Warbasse Designs, who specializes in Mobile Marketing tagging campaigns for an industry-leading clientele.

11. *http://www.unitaglive.com - UnitagLive is France's best export ever, as far as I'm concerned. Instantly create luscious Designer QR Codes, or full-featured Mobile-Optimized Landing pages. Just expect to have to pay in Euros.*
12. *http://www.beqrio.us*
13. *http://www.qrlicious.com*
14. *http://www.qrstuff.com - My all-time favorite QR Generation service. A true business asset. Encode 20 types of data formats in your codes, shorten with their integral shortener, choose your colors, manage all your codes through their desktop, unique features like re-assignable AKA "dynamic" QR Codes, or use a bulk upload to generate codes (or simply shorten URLs).*

26. Materials

Download the most current version of all of our materials in Adobe Acrobat .PDF format at http://eshlepper.com/materials.

QR Code Campaign Design Checklist

1. *Is there an adequate "Call to Action?"*
2. *Does the QR Code Explicitly Say Scan Me with Your Smart Phone? (or words to that EXACT effect)*
3. *Is there an adequate explanation the QR Code's presence? (Purpose of QR Code? Why should I scan this? Where does this link to? What is the next step?)*
4. *Is there a recommended place to download a scanner application?*
5. *Is there an easy-to-type alternative text-URL response link for non-scanners? (This need not be the same URL)*
6. *Is the Landing Page unique to this campaign?*
7. *Is there useful data being collected on the scanners/visitors?*
8. *Is there an alternate response URL for non-scanners?*
9. *Is the above short & easy to type?*
10. *Is your campaign Landing Page submitted to search engines?*
11. *Is Landing Page Useful? Fun? Content is King!*
12. *Is your URL Shortened?*
13. *Is URL Shortener re-directable? For re-use of code?*
14. *Or Last-Resort Campaign Rescue?*
15. *Is the web page response being tracked?*
16. *Google Analytics? Metrics through URL-Shortening Service?*
17. *Is other response being tracked?*
18. *Are custom color/design elements used for QR Code?*
19. *Does the QR Code Explicitly Say Scan Me?*
20. *Include URL for QR Code Scanner App Download?*
21. *Is there a Social Media Share option?*
22. *Automated Social Media Interactions?*
23. *Is there a reason to engage & communicate?*
24. *Is there a means to engage & communicate? Web-Form? Phone? Email?*
25. *Are friendly shorteners employed?*
26. *Are Variable or dynamic QR Codes employed?*

27. References

Books & Periodicals

"Information technology – Automatic identification and data capture techniques – QR Code 2005 bar code symbology specification," International Standards Organization (ISO), 2nd Edition, 1 September, 2006.

Waters, Joe, "QR Codes for Dummies", John Wiley & Sons Publishers, Hoboken, NJ, 2012.

Williams, George, 'The Quick Response Code – Strategic Marketing Tool, or Simply a Fad?", 2012

The Flyer, Carrollwood/Northdale (Greater Tampa) Edition, April 17, 2013, p1.

Liebowitz, Matt, "QR Codes Can Be Rigged To Attach Smart Phones, ScientificAmerican.com. September 13, via http://www.scientificamerican.com/

White Papers & Fact Sheets

"Getting Ahead of the Emerging QR Code Marketing Trend", Pitney Bowes, Jan 2013

"2011 QR Code Creation & Data Usage Trends Report" QRStuff.com

Google, Multiple Sites

"How to Go Mobile" – Google Corporation, 2012.

Friedman, Diana, "10 Truths of Mobile Tagging with QR Codes", Tappinn.com, 28 Oct, 2011

"Getting ahead of the emerging QR Code marketing trend", Pitney Bowes, Ltd, 2012 http://www.pitneybowes.com

"Microsoft© Tag Implementation Guide", Microsoft Corporation, Dec 2011

"Google Glass: What it Does." Google, 2013

Websites & Online Articles

"Report Shows Record 18 Million Mobile Barcode Scans in Q1 2013" http://www.ScanLife.com, April 30, 2013

"Global Growth in Mobile Barcode Usage – Q3 / 2011"http://www.i-nigma.com, October 10, 2011

Microsoft Corporation, multiple locations

27. *http://tag.microsoft.com/resources/implementation-guide.aspx*
28. *"Creating Custom Tags", Microsoft Corporation, July 2011 http://tag.microsoft.com/libraries/downloadable_documents/*

29. *http://www.google.com/glass/start/what-it-does/*

DENSO WAVE INCORPORATED, multiple sites.

30. *Denso ADC, "QR Code Essentials", 2011*
31. *http://www.QRCode.com*
32. *http://www.denso-wave.com*
33. *http://www.qrcode.com/en/faqpatent.html*

Wikipedia: The Online Encyclopedia, various articles:

34. *http://en.wikipedia.org/wiki/QR_Code*
35. *http://en.wikipedia.org/wiki/Shot_Code*
36. *http://en.wikipedia.org/wiki/Data_Matrix*
37. *http://en.wikipedia.org/wiki/URL_shortening*
38. *http://en.wikipedia.org/wiki/ShotCode*

Happy Birthday UPC: 35th Anniversary of the Bar Code, 1 June, 2009, http://www.gs1us.org/about-gs1-us/media-center/gs1-us-press-releases/happy-birthday-u.p.c.-thirty-fifth-anniversary-o

http://searchengineland.com/analysis-which-url-shortening-service-should-you-use-17204

http://www.cnet.com/news/qr-codes-arent-useless-after-all-nielsen-study-says/

NEC's Infamous Case of Identity Theft:

http://www.nytimes.com/2006/05/01/technology/01pirate.html?pagewanted=all&_r=0

"QR Codes Go to College", Archrival, 2011. http://www.archrival.com http://archrival.com/ideas/13/qr-codes-go-to-college

39. *http://www.QRStuff.com, 2012*
40. *http://www.iso.org*
41. *http://www.meyerweb.com/eric/tools/dencoder/*
42. *http://www.securelist.com/en/blog/208193145/*
43. *http://www.CustomQRCodes.com/custom-qr-codes-gallery*
44. *http://www.BeQRious.com/custom-qr-codes*
45. *http://www.eMarketer.com*
46. *http://www.Print2D.com*

Photo & Image Credits

True Blood QR Code, by Warbasse Designs © 2011 Warbasse Media, us*ed with permission*

Olive Garden QR Code, scanned and re-touched from disposable drink coasters used at the restaurant, 2011.

Food & Vegetable QR Code inspired by QR Code seen at http://www.qrtuning.com

Cover Image created at Wordle.net

All other images and photos unlisted are © 2013 Daniel Benjamin, and may be used with permission, by citing as "© 2013 Daniel Benjamin, http://Eshlepper.com"

28. Trademarks

All references to trademarks, including but not limited to the following, are the property of their respective owners:

Coca-Cola, Coke, Denso Wave Incorporated, QR Code, Amazon, Microsoft, Microsoft Tag, Windows, Adobe, Adobe Photoshop, Flash, Adobe Flash, Home Box Office, HBO, Citibank, Shotcode, Blotcode, Wimo, Apple, iPad, iPod, Kindle, Nook, Samsung, Samsung Galaxy, FHM Magazine, Cosmopolitan, The Sun, Sanyo, Kyocera, Motorola, Nokia, NEC, Toshiba, Hitachi, Samsung, Sharp, LG, Sony Ericsson & Casio, YOURLS, Hostgator, Godaddy, Bluehost, Nokia, T9, Calvin Klein & Calvin Klein X, Data Matrix Code, PDF417, Data Matrix, DotCode, Blotcode, Shotcode, UPC, Universal Product Code, Adobe Acrobat/Photoshop/LiveCycle Manager, Formstack, Wufoo.

29. About the Author

Daniel J. Benjamin has worked in Direct Mail, Social Media & Online Marketing for more than 30 years, having started out developing websites and ecommerce as a teenager. He's applied his marketing talents to multiple industries, including real estate, automotive dealer marketing, restaurants, e-commerce solutions, consumer lending, mortgage marketing, as well as insurance sales and the not-for-profit sector.

His winning strategies in marketing come from a convergence of his psychological studies, years of experience within the United States Postal Service, direct mail & even the military intelligence field, as well as direct-response and lead generation & tracking using Landing Pages, Interactive Voice Response systems, QR Codes & eMail marketing campaigns in his work on mail piece, ad design, as well incorporating highly data-driven direct response tracking to campaigns that he operates. He is currently the President of eShlepper Marketing, and personally oversees online, print media & direct mail marketing campaigns for select clients from his office in Boynton Beach, Florida.

Daniel is an alumnus of the State College of Florida & the University of South Florida, and the proud father and stepfather of five. When he's not building revenue for clients, he can be found in his workshop, clumsily turning large pieces of wood into smaller pieces of wood, with loads of bandages and anti-coagulants close at hand.

He has operated a number of blogs of note related to his other interests (usually under pseudonyms).

30. Afterword

In closing, thanks for joining me on this journey and reading. I hope that this has all been as edifying as possible, and at least as much so as was promised. By all means, visit my blog at http://Eshlepper.com/ and participate in the ongoing discussions.

Technology and certainly anything web-related is a difficult topic to write about, as there is simply too much information out there. Anyone with an opinion is free to contribute his own two cents, and present it with all the credibility and seeming authority of a seasoned expert in the field.

More importantly, technology and the Internet is also difficult to write about because they are perpetually in flux. Since I first determined to write these chapters, and throughout the four months of research & writing, various information has changed. Technology has matured. My preferred QR Code technologies and services shuffled several times. Items on which I'd written entire sections (or even a chapter or two) have been entirely obsoleted. Completely omitted topics have been thrust to the fore.

Further, my own understanding of the subject matter has evolved. Some of the authorities I've spoken to, most notably Philip Warbasse, have dramatically altered my understanding of the topics at hand, and greatly steered the material off the course I had initially plotted for this tome; for example, I had intended to omit much about Mobile Marketing and Mobile Optimization, topics which are too integral to omit. As a deadline passes, with three chapters yet to research (and four new chapters suddenly deemed necessary), there comes a time when one realizes that to write everything about a topic and expect it to be up-to-date is an impossibility… because between the time the first copy sells and the 1,000th copy sells, much of the information may be somewhat out of date, superseded by information in the Nth chapter that one didn't even know to write at the time.

Thus, to be sure, this isn't the book I intended to write. This is not the book that I would have written six months ago, and it certainly isn't the book that I'd write six months from now. It can only be the book I wrote today. Projects take on lives of their own, and eventually one must realize that the only way to get the entire story right, perfect, and complete, is to write it retrospectively, from hundreds of years in the future, explaining the dead, cold past as how it was, and how everyone knows it to be.

To write, in the present, about the present, is a daunting task, indeed. Surely, this is why eBook formats and Blogging have become so ubiquitous in technical and internet circles, because of their speed – by the time anything of substantial length (or printed on paper) can be created in any quantity, it may be almost outdated. At some point, an author must draw a line of demarcation between that which can be written now, and that which must come in a latter installment.

That line of demarcation, for this book, is here: ______________________________

FIN

31. Index

The Ultimate Guide to Mobile Marketing with QR Codes:

The Definitive Strategy Manual for Winning Marketing with QR Codes

By Daniel J. Benjamin

2nd Edition, October 2024

Questions? Email qr@eshlepper.com

ISBN#: 978-1-960282-05-7

See also:

eBook on Amazon Kindle Marketplace

Full-color edition: 978-1-960282-06-4

Hardcover: Coming soon

www.ingramcontent.com/pod-product-compliance
Lightning Source LLC
LaVergne TN
LVHW060140070326
832902LV00018B/2884